THE SCANDALOUS GHOST

THE SCANDALOUS GHOST

Sartre's Existentialism as Related to
Vitalism, Humanism, Mysticism, Marxism

by Jacques L. Salvan

Wayne State University Press, Detroit, 1967

To Alain Serdac

CONTENTS

PREFACE

An Encounter

*The layman who asks an authority to define existen-
tialism is likely to be told that it is a philosophical technique and
a difficult one. If the thought occurs to him that, as an existent,
he is entitled to some curiosity as to the meaning of his existence,
he may seek his initiation in a public lecture; there he may learn
that God is dead, that man is alone in a meaningless world, and
that everything is absurd, or else that he exists authentically only
when facing God in fear and trembling. He is also likely to learn
much about the existence of such people as Kierkegaard, Kafka,
Camus, Heidegger, or Sartre, but very little about his own beyond
the vague notion that it precedes his "essence." He is also likely
to come out with the conviction that existentialism is a philosophy
to end philosophy.*

*If, pursuing his quest, he consults the works of the main
existentialists, he is then referred to Hegel, Descartes, Plato and
the pre-Socratic philosophers. Far from bearing directly on his
own confused world, existentialism seems to find its roots in the
most distant past, and is in some way related to metaphysical
systems that modern philosophy was supposed to have buried. By
comparison, James and Bergson read like poetry.*

*In particular, an initiation to Sartre is something of an intro-
duction to the less popular chapters in the history of philosophy.*

I found it as rewarding as it was laborious and thought—this was at a time when popular reviews treated existentialism as the latest expression of Left Bank bohemianism—that what I had learned was worth communicating to other existents in quest of existentialism. A few doubts, concerning the exact meaning to be attributed to certain terms and the exact relationship of the new philosophy to other modes of thought, made it desirable for me to solicit from Sartre the interview which I am about to relate, as I wrote it down from memory shortly afterwards for a student publication:

No. 47 rue Bonaparte, the placid concierge at the end of the hallway, the four flights of narrow stairway, had that most ordinary look of ageless wear common to modest hotels, but the study into which I have just been introduced seems stamped with the distinction of ancient Parisian districts by its paneling of a watery pale green. Is this Mathieu's study, I wonder, that green room suffused with the intellectual fluidity of perpetual refusal of self-commitments? The high window opens on the square of Saint-Germain-des-Prés, of provincial calm on this summer Sunday. On the left, I see bookshelves behind a long desk on which I notice a few pipes and a grey package of plain tobacco—from a passage of *L'Etre et le Néant*, I had come to believe that Sartre had given up the symbolic destruction of the world in his pipe bowls—on the right, other shelves, one or two art objects; in the back, a couch covered with a sort of tiger-skin. I look at the titles of the books on the shelves at my right: all history books. I had seen Sartre appear on the screen the day before; he was being interviewed, his answers came out, high-pitched, sharp and quick as machine-gun fire . . .

The door opens. I feel protected by the fact that I am standing against the light and by my being a complete stranger, an unknown quantity. Sartre steps forward in full light and I have the immediate impression of a modesty which borders on shyness. Toward him a whole world flows back, the world in which he made me live, with so many of my contemporaries. Very cordially, he shakes hands and leads me, between the window and the desk, to the captivity of a low and narrow green arm-chair, asks me if I smoke and hands me a cigarette as thick as a forefinger, then sits opposite me. I state as precisely as I can the subject of the interview he is granting me: a detailed summary, in English, of *L'Etre et le Néant*. There is no translation of this work. The reviews which have been given—we are in 1951—are rather superficial and even erroneous. Most of them neglect a point which seems essential to me: the negative character of consciousness. He approves. Does he have, to begin with, any objection to works of popularization?

"None. *There is no definite formulation of ideas.* They gain by being thought over. They are clarified, or enriched, by the light projected on them by different minds."

"It is sometimes difficult to incorporate them otherwise than in the original form, hardly modified, even when one is not quoting."

"This practice is accepted in philosophy."

"I thank you. Now I should like to ask a few questions on some basic notions, so as to be sure not to betray your thought."

"Please do."

"Non-being comes from being?"

"Yes."

"But is not that being which already contains non-being a synthesis of being and non-being?"

"In phenomenology, one has to see things and to describe them as they appear to consciousness. From a metaphysical viewpoint, consciousness as pure non-being must be *the result of a long process of disaggregation* within being."

"Liberty in your work is identified with consciousness. I do not see very well what place Life has in it. Doesn't Life already represent the striving toward indeterminacy?"

"I do not deny Life. But how are you going to study it in itself? Either you study it from outside as one dissects a corpse and it is no longer life, or else you identify it with the consciousness you have of it . . . You would have to invent a method, a technique . . ."

"It is true that life is not consciousness, does not start with it, and eventually can admirably dispense with it . . ."

I express my wonder that one may continue to live, act, and speak for hours and days in a state of complete unconsciousness. "To what extent then does the consciousness of others become one's own?" With his conciliatory manner, his way of encouraging you in your views, this man seems to lead you to think aloud. I confess that, in spite of all, I have kept my respect for Bergson.

"I have nothing against Bergson. I just reproach him with being *chosiste*."* How can his interpenetration of 'states of consciousness' or his 'deeper ego' create liberty? What does he mean with his 'duration'?"

"One does not know how it can mean change if it is mere persistence of states of consciousness?"

"Exactly."

"To pass to another question: are there not certain connections between existentialism and mysticism?"

"I have nothing against mysticism except that it seeks outside of consciousness *a unity that does not exist.*"

"Mysticism proclaims, *That Art Thou*; your existentialism, *That Art Thou Not.* Am I mistaken?"

Sartre seems amused and altogether pleased but he does not answer.

"Could not one trace back your idea of a 'detotalized totality' to a certain romantic nature mysticism? Have you read Poe's *Eureka?*"

"A long time ago; I have no clear recollection of it."

---

* A favorite neologism of Sartre which might perhaps be translated as: "tending to *thinghood*," or "*thingification*."

"It seems to me that in *Eureka* I have come across something similar to this denial of the unity of Mind that you were expressing a moment ago; a denial which involves the notion of a 'detotalized totality.' Is not the fragmentation of Mind into a multiplicity of consciousnesses what you wanted to express by the very technique of *The Reprieve?*"

"Why yes, indeed."

"It is also, if I understand rightly, the basic idea of *No Exit.* May I ask a question concerning that play? . . . Your hell appears at first under the aspect of a thesis concerning the survival of consciousness, then, more closely considered, as an allegory of existence. Could it be that it is neither one nor the other but rather an abstract scheme for the presentation of an idea? You do away with time and the world to confront consciousnesses without a future and demonstrate their essential character and incompatibility . . ."

"Why yes. You remember that admirable page of Husserl . . ."

I do not know the admirable page of Husserl, but Sartre does not even give me time to confess my ignorance. The tone of his voice has gone up, his manner has become more categorical. I have completely ceased following him, and missed my chance to know the source of *No Exit.*

"One last question on *No Exit,* a question of dramatic technique. This play had given me the impression that we were going back to the Racinian drama of crisis and concentration, but I just saw *Lucifer and the Good Lord,* which follows the pattern of the Elizabethan drama of development. How did you pass from one technique to the other?"

"I consider that *form has no importance except in relation to demonstration.* I chose in both cases the form best adapted to what I wanted to say."

Having gone through the questions I was determined to ask, I realize that I enjoy this conversation prodigiously. At once

13

a scruple comes to me against taking further advantage of the "corrupting arm-chair" and of the intellectual comfort some character of *The Age of Reason* used to find in it.

Now that we are standing, I find it hard to leave this man who has not once departed from his cordiality and intellectual generosity.

"I believe that the American public, still unable to follow your dialectics, is mostly interested in your work for its ethical implications. If individual consciousness is an absolute, there is undoubtedly no hope of harmony between consciousnesses on the plane of being?"

"*None.*"

"But every hope is permitted on the plane of doing?"

"Yes, and also, what people do not clearly understand is that *the absolute character of one's consciousness involves reciprocity.*"

This is, on the part of the author of *No Exit,* a precious concession, and one which I do not remember having encountered in his works.

"In regard to the ethical question, I recommend to you Jeanson's *Le Problème moral et la pensée de Sartre* as interpreting my views to my complete satisfaction. You don't have a copy? Wait . . ."

He searches in vain through a few shelves.

"I thought I had one. I'll tell my secretary to send you one. To what address in Paris?"

"I am leaving to-morrow."

"I am also leaving . . . Could it not be left somewhere until your return? . . . In a café, for instance? Or else, telephone my secretary when you come back . . . and if you need some information, bibliographical or other, don't hesitate to write . . ."

The little square of Saint-Germain-des-Prés is bathed in the clear afternoon sun of early summer, but that even and transparent light respects the color of things like a lucid consciousness. Could not the harmony of souls become realizable in that light as well as in the team spirit?

My quest must be pursued with the few indications I have just received. What does Sartre's existentialism have in common with other philosophies of Existence? As a philosophy of liberty, what are its relations with the philosophy of Life? As a form of humanism, how does it fit in with the humanist tradition? As a denial of mystical postulates, could it be that it is historically related to these postulates, either directly, or as a challenge to the unifying vision of the mystic, who seeks the unity of the universe in transcendental symbolism, and to whom the multiplicity of consciousnesses is a scandalous illusion? The following essays were written at long intervals to clarify these questions.

To Symposium *and* The French Review, *for permission to make use of some previously published material, to Barbara Woodward for excellent suggestions concerning the final composition of this work, the author's thanks are due.*

J. L. S.

1

Introduction
Existentialism as the "Situated Cogito"

Sartre's statement: "Existence precedes essence" is probably the most commonly quoted definition of existentialism; yet its meaning is vague to the layman, questionable to some philosophers of existence, misinterpreted by others, as the terms "existence," "precedes," and "essence" are variously understood. Within its context, Sartre's formula refers only to human existence. Blake's "tyger, burning bright in the forest of the night," may owe its existence to some thought, dream, or improvisation of God, nature, or creative evolution, which constitutes its essence, or nature; as the manifestation of this essence, the existing tiger must follow its nature, which is its tigerness. But man, according to Sartre, creates his own essence, or nature, which simply means that he is free and that what he is results from what he does. But, even with Sartre, this is more of a conclusion than it is a basic philosophical position; Sartre starts with the quest of Being.

The definition of existentialism as "the philosophy of the Here and Now" offers a preferable point of departure; for existentialism is not just an attitude or a mood, as is often suggested, but a philosophy of the traditional sort, concerned with the quest of an absolute, and bearing to a large extent on the great philosophies of the past; yet, at the same time, and in keeping with the trend of modern science, it is a philosophy which tries to account at once for the observer and the world observed, starts from the situation of the observer in time and space, and carries on its quest from that plane, which is the plane of existence.

It is, as we shall see, because the existentialist insists on pursuing his quest from the plane of existence—which the average philosopher likes to leave behind as soon as possible—that existentialism may be called a structure. Of course, you do not need to be a philosopher to question the ultimate meaning of your existence; many novelists, playwrights, and artists have done so in our times. But in the tension which generally results from the attempt to integrate one's personal existence within a cosmic vision, they have seldom gone beyond the feelings of absurdity and anguish. For this reason, Kafka, Malraux, and Camus should, in my opinion, be called "existential" rather than "existentialist" writers.

As a philosopher, the existentialist is supposed to make some sense out of the absurdity of existence, and relate it to Being. Unlike the scientist, the philosopher can take nothing for granted, which is what Valéry meant by stating that science consists in pretending that you know what you do not know, and philosophy in pretending that you do not know what you know. The first statement may or may not apply to modern science, but it is a fact that one of the most arduous tasks facing the traditional philosopher is to prove the reality of his existence and of the world around him or, to use his own expression, "to get out of solipsism." This is not as easy as it seems. Among the arguments which Greek philosophy delighted in working out from close analysis of movement, multiplicity, and time, to prove that existence is an illusion, the well-known Heraclitean paradox concerning time will suffice for our purpose: the past is no more, the future is not yet, and present, closely considered, immediately splits between past and future, which proves that we really are not at any time. Montaigne, who developed this argument among others during his skeptic mood, concluded that God alone *Is,* outside of time, space, and change. Such reasoning, on a purely philosophical plane, leads to the distinction between *Existence,* which really *Is Not,* and *Being,* which *Does Not Exist,* since it is outside of space, time and change.

2. THE "COGITO" SITUATED ON THE PLANE OF CONTEMPLATION

It is to such, or similar, arguments that Descartes answered: "I shall grant you that existence may be an appearance, an illusion, or a dream, and will therefore cast systematic doubt on the reality of everything that I ever took for granted; but you cannot deny me that if I doubt, I think, and that if I think, I am: *Cogito, ergo sum;* I am, at least insofar as I think, as a "thinking substance." For the first time, the conscious self, in all its subjectivity, asserts itself as the starting point of philosophy; but now, if I am only as a "thinking substance," in fact a sort of anonymous consciousness, unrelated with the world which it has left behind, the world itself may still be my dream. Has Cartesian thought tried in vain to lift itself, as it were, by its boot straps? Immediately, Descartes realizes that doubting implies the idea of imperfection, which in turn implies the idea of perfection; and since everything I know, including my doubting self, is imperfect, this idea of perfection could have no other source than a perfect Being, who is God. From the idea of a perfect Being, who could not deceive us, Descartes derives the reality of the world, which appears to him as space, or extension. He can now proceed to translate extension into algebra and mathematics, i.e. into thought, with the help of his coordinates. The thinking substance, as a center of reference, is no more than the abstract point where his coordinates meet. Descartes ends in a sort of dualism where the world of thought and the world of space are, in some way, mysteriously joined, yet completely distinct.

This is acceptable, perhaps, on the plane of scientific knowledge. But, as Huxley remarks, science never tells us anything about what we are really interested in: the meaning of our existence. Descartes' *cogito,* according to the existentialists, is to be commended for starting with the conscious self, but this conscious self is divorced from concrete existence. It represents the effort of consciousness to become conscious of itself as such, without any reference to the world in which it finds itself situated; but before it can doubt the reality of the world, consciousness finds itself facing that world, or, to use William James' expression, "at the edge of the world," in fact, inseparable from the world.

To place the *cogito:* "I think, therefore I am," within the Here and Now is precisely what Descartes' contemporary, Pascal, tried to do. Before thought can think itself as a pure abstraction, it discovers itself as a center of reference determined by the existence of a body situated in the world between two infinites of greatness and smallness, infinitely removed from the beginning and the end of things, which alone would permit man to understand his situation, unable to understand the absurd contingency of its existence here rather than there. This discovery is not made through the clear and distinct ideas of discursive thought, but rather through these revealing emotions that we will find again in modern existentialism. The very fact, however, that existence may appear contingent and absurd is a proof that there is in man an element that is neither contingent nor absurd. Pascal's reasoning can be compared to Descartes' discovery of God, as logical necessity, in the notion of perfection; but Pascal's self-awareness is a pre-reflective *cogito,* existentially situated. The realization of man's situation—which is the human condition—and the sense of an absolute Being, which makes of that situation a determinate being, cannot be separated.

3. THE "COGITO" SITUATED ON THE PLANE OF BECOMING

We must now return to the notion of Being, such as we encounter it in Hegel's objective idealism. Hegel's picture of man's "unhappy consciousness" does not differ essentially from Pascal's description of man's "misery and greatness"; but Hegel derives from that opposition the conclusion that consciousness has access to all Reality on the plane of Reason. From the study, (in his Phenomenology) of the structures of consciousness, Hegel raises himself (in his Logic) to the level of absolute Being. This notion of an absolute, or pure, Being, which is neither *this*, nor *that*, nor anything imaginable, seems to vanish, when you consider it closely, into that of pure Nothingness. As in logic, so in Hegel's universe, Being, a pure idea, generates its opposite, Non-Being, and the two combined constitute Becoming. Thus, the Heraclitean contention that there is nothing in this world that does not contain at once being and non-being receives its justification on a purely idealistic plane. Each individual consciousness represents only one moment in the becoming of the World-Mind. There is, therefore, no truth except as understood from the viewpoint of the Totality; or, rather, Totality is Universal Truth, and our own individual truth is in its relation to Totality, as the truth of the paragraph is in the complete book. While Hegel's conception of the world as Idea does violence to common sense, it is actually harder to disprove on closer analysis than pure materialism. Furthermore, idealism lends itself particularly well to a dialectical system through the very dynamism of ideas.

Kierkegaard is to Hegel what Pascal is to Descartes. He claims that to adopt the point of view of the Totality, we should have to be outside of it. Again it is a question of reestablishing the individual consciousness as the center of reference; truth is not Totality, truth is subjective intensity. To Kierkegaard, it is not the World-Mind which is in process of becoming through human consciousness, it is the existing subject himself who is in process of becoming, the finite self facing the infinite Self, whose call he has to answer every moment with "Yes" or "No." Kierkegaard's protest was against the totalitarian idealism of his age as modern existentialism is a protest against the materialistic or biological view of the totality in ours.

4. THE "COGITO" SITUATED ON THE PLANE OF ACTION

We may say, however, that modern philosophies of existence would be unthinkable if they had not been preceded by the philosophies of life represented by Nietzsche, William James, and Bergson. Nietzsche also proclaimed, in substance, that individual consciousness is the absolute center of reference, but since, with Nietzsche, God is dead, it is to the World as Will that the self has to answer every moment with "Yes" or "No." William James's pragmatism defined reality as a structure in which object and subject, the observer and the world observed, cannot be dissociated, and truth as that which can only be proven in action. Bergson established his famous distinction between the intelligence of *homo faber,* primarily intended to act on inorganic matter, and intuition which is, as immediate self-knowledge, the original impulse of life recaptured. These elements of the philosophies of life reappear in modern philosophies of existence. In them, particularly, the Bergsonian conception of the world as a complex of tools, on the plane of active participation, tends to replace the Pascalian world of contemplation and the silence of its infinite spaces, or the Hegelian world of universal becoming. The center of reference, however, is shifted from the biological plane of life and creative evolution to the concrete situation of the existing consciousness in the Here and Now.

This situation is defined by Martin Buber, in terms of subject-object relationships, as the *I-It* and the *I-Thou* planes of existence, the *I* remaining a permanent element in the two structures. The *I-It* plane corresponds to the Bergsonian conception of the world as a complex of tools, extended so as to include not only things, but others, and even God, as objects to be used for a purpose. The *I-Thou* plane, corresponding to intuitive knowledge, is the plane of realization; the *Thou,* as the other subject, may be the other person, God, and, in some strange mystical way, the world. In Buber, then, the philosophy of life receives a sort of mystical extension and is shifted to the *I* as a permanent center of reference.

At about the same time, the "concrete philosophy" of Gabriel Marcel develops, along somewhat similar lines, on the two planes of *Having* and *Being*. Taking the conscious self, situated in the universe through incarnation in a body, as a center of reference, he comes to realize that the sight, or thought, of any object is always related, no matter how indirectly, to the possibility of acting upon it through the body. When we can act on an object without restriction, we say that we *have* that object. Because we use our body to act upon it, we come to consider our body as a tool that we have; so do we other people when we use them, our own convictions when we say we *have* convictions, the very questions we raise when we say we *have* problems. Thus *Having* becomes a sort of degradation of participation in *Being*. Being is not a problem that I have, but a mystery that I am. Unfortunately, a mystery must be turned into a problem to be elucidated, in the same way as Bergsonian intuition needs intelligence to raise the question that will turn it into knowledge.

Karl Jaspers, whose philosophy appeared in 1932, also starts with the realization of a concrete situation which he calls the *Dasein,* or *being-there,* and which is comparable to Buber's *I-It* structure, as the plane of objective and scientific knowledge. To this plane, he opposes the plane of *Existenz,* which concerns man as subject, i.e. as a being that *is not,* but *can* and *must* be, and transcends the world as possibility and liberty. The transcendent reality toward which this movement is directed can only be defined negatively.

Closer to Bergson's philosophy of life and to pure mysticism, Berdyaev does not start with the concrete situation of the self in the Here and Now in such an explicit way. The self, as center of reference is, however, present in his conception of the *person,* spirit become conscious and sharing with God a liberty originating in the Naught anterior to creation.

In all the religious philosophies of existence we have considered, the finite self, taken as center of reference, is related to an infinite Self, or absolute *Thou.* With the disciples of Husserl: Heidegger and Sartre, the structure of existentialism becomes secularized. Husserl is not an existentialist, according to our definition, inasmuch as he does not go back to that immediate awareness of the conscious self facing the Here and Now which we have called the *"situated cogito,"* but prefers to stay on the plane of universal doubt which precedes the *cogito:* "I doubt, therefore I think," "bracketing the world," and leaving its reality in suspense through his "phenomenological reduction." Not satisfied with merely "bracketing" the world, like Descartes, so that the Ego might remain as consciousness, Husserl brackets consciousness itself, and claims access to an anonymous, or transcendental, consciousness from which to study its structure. Husserl's influence on modern existentialism consists mainly in a method allowing his disciples the minimum amount of detachment required to study the structures of consciousness from the most subjective viewpoint.

With Heidegger, realization by consciousness of its situation in the Here and Now is again called *Dasein,* or *being-there.* It is experienced directly in care, anguish, and *Geworfenheit,* the feeling of having been thrown into this situation without any known reason. Consciousness does not feel alone in this situation; it is also *Mitsein,* being-with-others. What Heidegger seems to add to this familiar picture is the "ek-static" character of consciousness, which involves a dimension of non-being. Man is not in the world like a stone or a tree; he is, so to speak, outside of himself, as if, through consciousness, he had taken a jump into nothingness to view his existence as a whole, between the non-being which preceded his birth and the nothingness which will follow his death, surrounded, within his life among the tool-complex of the world, by the ocean of things left undone. Authentic existence is assumed as a whole, between the non-being before birth and the nothingness of death. Our birth just happened, but we can give meaning to our death. *Being-for-death,* then, is authentic existence. Authentic temporality starts from the future, which is my project in the light of being-for-death, assumes the past, and acts in the present, with others. Inauthentic existence consists, generally, in forgetting our possibilities in in-authentic time, which is a succession of "nows," or tending to identify ourselves with the interchangeable and inexistent human being whom we call "one," "they," "people," and whom Heidegger calls *"das man."* Heidegger's quest of Being seems to have ended in an encounter with Non-Being. Being-in, being-with, and being-for are not Being, but limitations of Being; and these limitations are negations which, in some ways, spring from Non-Being. For, according to Heidegger, Non-Being is not what you get by negating *this* and *that* and everything imaginable. To the contrary, it is negation which derives from Non-Being: Non-Being nihilates.

Jean-Paul Sartre took full advantage of this innovation from the start. His starting-point is that of all other existentialists: the situation of the conscious self in the Here and Now; but this conscious self, as pre-reflective *cogito,* is, from the beginning, negation of identity with the object and remains such, whether the object is that of perception, consciousness itself, the other, or the world; so that consciousness, which has no being of its own, except *for itself,* is, in last analysis, an absolute negation identical with absolute Non-Being. In opposition to Bergson, however, Sartre refuses to consider absolute Non-Being as the result of absolute negation. To him, as to Heidegger, it is negation which springs from the non-being at the very core of man's being. It must be that consciousness, or *being-for-itself,* is nothing else than the irruption of Non-Being into the world of Being. Since you cannot establish a cause-to-effect relation between Being and

Non-Being, since, in other words, you cannot say that something produces nothing, it must be that the nihilating power of consciousness as absolute negation is the origin of man's liberty.

We may then conclude that, as the philosophy of the conscious self situated in the Here and Now, existentialism throws light on the very structure of existence by distinguishing, and correlating in it, two planes, in the light, or on the background, of some absolute Being or, as in the case of Sartre, of an absolute Non-Being. As a philosophy which stresses the self, whether as an absolute, or directly related to an absolute, existentialism is perhaps not the main trend of our times, but rather a reaction against that trend. Its message is primarily to denounce an all too prevalent tendency toward objectification of the self, whether our own or the other's self, as well as any claim of mystical, or semi-mystical claim of unitive fusion of the self with the cosmos, or with God.

For a closer analysis of Sartre's ontology, the reader is referred to my *To Be and Not To Be,** and for a more comprehensive summary of the existentialist tradition, to the *Introduction* of that work, parts of which have been retained here, in a very condensed form, for the convenience of the reader unfamiliar with the previous work, the present series of essays being intended as its critical sequel.

* Detroit, Wayne State University Press, 1962.

2

Existentialism and Vitalism[1]

Bestriding the positive solid reality to which it
is attached, this phantom objectifies itself.

HENRI BERGSON

I. THE HERACLITEAN TRADITION
AND THE MODERN WORLD

Of the two philosophies which have done most to
rehabilitate the concept of liberty in our century, one seeks its
justification in the continuity of the mental process, the other in
its discontinuity; this paradox immediately faces us as we try
to relate Sartre's philosophy of Existence with Bergson's philosophy of Life.

Both philosophies are basically intuitive and rely on imagery
whenever the conceptual vocabulary seems lacking in suggestive
power; both are, in some ways, related to the Heraclitean philosophy of flux and change. The Heraclitean tradition which, up
to Hegel, had appeared in western thought—and mostly in liter-
ture—only to reenforce the Platonic stress on the unreality of human life, seems to have become one of the main streams of
modern thought. It reappears, unnamed, in the vitalistic trends of
the beginning of our century. Surrealism claims Heraclitus as its
distant precursor; Marxism, through Hegel, however misunder-
stood, might make the same claim. Existentialism through Kier-

kegaard, like Marx a rebellious disciple of Hegel, remains indebted to Hegelian dialectics. This indebtness is particularly apparent in Sartre. Some Hegelian themes, conveniently summed
up for us by Josiah Royce, might almost serve us as an introductory outline of the questions raised by *L'Etre et le Néant*:

> Each one of us is what some other moment of his life reflectively
> finds him to be . . . No one of us knows what he now is; he can
> only know what he *was*. Each one of us, however, is *now* only
> what hereafter he *shall* find himself to be. . . . We get self-
> possession, self-apprehension, self-knowledge, only through end-
> lessly fleeing from ourselves, and then turning back to look at
> what we were. But this paradox relates not only to moments. It
> relates to all life. . . . All feeling, all character, all thought, all
> life, exists for us only in so far as it can be reflected upon, viewed
> from without, seen at a distance, acknowledged by another than
> itself, reworded in terms of fresh experience. Stand still where you
> are, stand alone, isolate your life, and forthwith you are nothing.
> Enter into relations, exist for the reflective thought of yourself,
> or of other people, criticise yourself and be criticised, observe your-
> self and be observed, exist, and at the same time look upon your-
> self and be looked upon from without, and then indeed you are
> somebody, a self with a consistency and a vitality, a being with a
> genuine life.[2]

We recognize in these lines the flight of the in-itself into the for-
itself, the mechanism of temporality through which it takes place,
the passage from the for-itself to the for-itself-for-others. With
Sartre, this constant flight away from ourselves does *not* lead to
the realization of the complete self. It merely represents the vain
effort of our contingent and absurd being to ground itself in
consciousness, whether our own, the other's, or God's. This attempt is doomed to failure because our being (in-itself) can only
become aware of itself through negating its identity. Consciousness remains separated from being by the non-being implied in
this negation. This break in the continuity of consciousness is
the instant, the meeting-point of the in-itself, become the past,
with the for-itself which constitutes itself into a free project.

Our consciousness, having no being of its own, can only subsist as a presence to that which it is not and can never become. We are not here concerned with the impossibility for consciousness to be reflected and acknowledged as such by another consciousness. Let us simply note that, like Hegel's *Mind,* Sartre's *consciousness* is a pure negativity produced by a mysterious non-being within our very being.

2. THE IDEA OF NON-BEING

Hegel, however, had merely juxtaposed the abstract notions of Being and Non-Being, to derive from that combination the idea of Becoming, without explaining the process. Sartre claims for himself the merit of having sought non-being in the very core of man's being.[3] One might say that, in this respect, he represents Hegel thought over from the viewpoint of Descartes' *cogito.* He rejects the conception of a world given, in its totality, as a synthesis of Being and Non-Being, and identifies the surge of Non-Being in the world with the awakening of man's consciousness; he dismisses the idea of universal Becoming, but retains the conception of a dialectical opposition between Being and Non-Being which, in his philosophy, is shifted to the plane of individual consciousness.

Bergson, on the contrary, seemed to have retained from the Heraclitean tradition the notion of eternal becoming but to have rejected that other Heraclitean principle according to which everything in this world is made up at once of being and non-being. Non-being figures in Bergson as a pseudo-idea, as a movement of the mind which posits the existence of a thing, then rejects it; or rather it is merely a form of substitution borrowed from the practical language:

"Nothing" is a term of the usual language which can only have meaning if we remain on the plane, peculiar to man, of action and fabrication. "Nothing" designates the absence of what we seek, of what we desire, of what we expect. Supposing, indeed, that experience should ever present us with an absolute void, it would be limited, it would have contours, it would still be something. But in reality there is no void. We perceive and even conceive only plenum. A thing disappears only because another has replaced it. Suppression means substitution. Only we say "suppression" when we envisage only one of the two halves, or rather of the two faces, of substitution: that which interests us; we thus stress that we are pleased to direct our attention to the departed object and turn it away from that which has replaced it.[4]

For Sartre, on the contrary:

. . . if there is being everywhere, it is not only non-being which, as Bergson claims, is inconceivable. The necessary condition for it being possible to say *no* is that non-being be a perpetual presence in us and around us, it is that non-being should haunt being.[5]

Negation could not be, as Bergson claims, reduced to the persistence of our attention to an object which has been replaced by another; or rather it is that attention which contains a series of negations: implicit negation of everything which is not that object—Sartre borrows from Spinoza the principle that every determination is a negation—negation of the existence of the object in the image retained by consciousness, negation of that very image by the consciousness which distinguishes itself from it.

Negation, to Sartre, is the very foundation of our liberty:

By conceiving, starting from my perceptions of the room which he inhabited, the person who is no longer in the room, I am in all necessity led to accomplish an act of thought which no anterior state can determine or motivate, briefly to operate within myself a break with being. . . . This break is precisely non-being.[6]

This break, or split, of non-being within being remains to be defined. To our surprise, it is not a complete break of continuity; Sartre approves Bergson for having rejected the conception of the instant as an indivisible temporal point. Neither is it "an opaque element which might have separated the anterior from the posterior state, as a knife's blade parts a fruit in two." [7] The anterior consciousness is still there, modified into a "past," "it still keeps up a relation of interpretation with the present consciousness," but it is, in some way, "outside of the game, outside of circuit, between parentheses. . . ." [8]

Bergson is not unaware of this negative moment, of this split in the continuity of our psychic life, but he considers it as a necessary illusion brought about by the very demands of action: "Just as we pass through the immobile to go to the moving, so we make use of the void to think the full." [9] As the negation of being, non-being benefits by the affirmation at the bottom of it. "Bestriding the positive solid reality to which it is attached, this phantom objectifies itself." [10]

> If now we analyze this idea of Nothing, we find that it is at bottom, the idea of Everything, together with a movement of the mind that keeps jumping from one thing to another, refuses to stand still, and concentrates all its attention on this refusal by never determining its actual position except by relation to that which it has just left.[11]

The "movement of the mind," by which the mind rejects every thing in turn, in order to reach the idea of absolute non-being, is only possible, according to Sartre, because the mind itself is, to start with, an absolute non-being: "Non-being grounds negation as an act because it is negation *as being*." [12] By rejecting *this* or *that,* the mind, or consciousness, an absolute negation, simply turns into a *qualified* negation of *this* and *that;* it always remains a negation. Furthermore, since the world, for us, is only the succession of what Bergson calls our "states of consciousness," consciousness is an internal negation. Bergson's phantom, bestriding the positive reality to which it is attached, is one with that reality, at once being and non-being. It may not quite succeed in objectifying itself, but it is at once the image of our non-being and that of our liberty. It cannot be as easily dismissed as Bergson would have us believe, for it is the source of our anguish.

3. ANGUISH, NON-BEING, AND FREEDOM

Anguish springs, according to Bergson, Kierkegaard, and Heidegger, from the idea of nothingness. For Sartre, it is merely the consciousness of liberty, but these two conceptions are not contradictory: "they imply each other. . . ." [13]

Bergson considers anguish on the intellectual plane, and concludes that it is the source of one of the pseudo-problems of philosophy: that which consists in wondering why there is being: "why something or somebody exists." According to him, that problem arises because we tend to imagine that non-being precedes being, an attitude suited to action and fabrication, but entirely out of place in philosophy:

> . . . when we move from the domain of fabrication to that of creation, when we wonder why there is being, why something or someone, why the world or God exists and why not nothingness, when we, in short, ask ourselves the most anguishing of metaphysical problems, we virtually accept an absurdity; for if any suppression is a substitution, if the idea of a suppression is merely the truncated idea of a substitution, then to speak of a substitution which would not be one is to contradict oneself. [14]

Questions about the origin of being, or about the origin of the world are equally devoid of meaning for Sartre, and for the same reason: they presuppose that non-being precedes being. They seem to contain a reference to the question: "why is there being?" to which he answers that consciousness causes the world to be there by dissociating itself from it, giving to the expression "there is" a phenomenological meaning: as the world appears to my consciousness, my consciousness experiences at once, through anguish, its non-being and its liberty. Dizziness is a concrete form of anguish: I feel dizzy before a precipice, not because I am afraid of falling into it but because I realize that nothing can prevent me from jumping over it; this is anguish before the future. I may experience anguish in regard to the past if I have decided never to gamble again and realize, as I approach the gambling table, that I am as desperately free to do so as ever, and that nothing can prevent me from changing my mind. By the very fact that I am conscious of my resolve, I have, in some way, gone beyond; I am past that resolve. I do not deny that I am the person who made the resolve, I preserve my identity, yet I do not completely identify my present consciousness with my past decision; that decision is *for me* to reassume or to reject. Deliberation is merely an attempt to find logical necessity in our behavior. Thus Hamlet, having decided that he has all the reasons in the world to kill the king, discovers equally good reasons not to do so when he finds him praying. Consciousness is a sort of constantly reborn self-questioning, and questioning always involves the possibility of a negation. If this is true, Bergson's conception of the free act as an act slowly and progressively coming to fruition through a long process of maturation is entirely to be rejected. His assertion that "suppression means substitution" is not valid in this case. The man who says: "I hate myself for having acted that way" feels sufficiently justified by mere disavowal of his behavior; a purely "negative behavior" is, as we all know, a fairly common pattern of human behavior. There are men in our society whose function consists merely in saying "no," and these living "no's" are satisfied with the rôle. Suppression for them does not mean substitution. It must be that man, as a conscious being, has a unique way of being and at once not being what he is.

4. LIBERTY, DURATION, TEMPORALITY

For Bergson, as we know, liberty proceeds from an interpenetration of all states of consciousness, which permits them to endure and become organized, thus allowing the *élan vital,* or life force, to utilize for its ends the energy of a material world characterized by the reciprocal exteriority of things. By relegating intensity and quantity, the basis of scientific determinism to the world of Matter, and by making of Mind the realm of quality, Bergson, after Descartes, sought in the unity of the thinking self the justification of our sense of liberty. The free act, in this conception, could be defined as representative of the Ego; it is the more free as it sums up more completely the Ego's history. It is precisely against the passive character of liberty thus understood that Sartre raises a protest: such liberty is the projection of real liberty into a psychic object, my inner self, which I refuse to consider as historically constituted; that liberty which would frighten me if I had to face it I attribute to a deeper self which dwells within me like a little God. I try to envisage it as if it were the liberty of someone else. Of course, my deeper self changes and transforms itself, but these changes are conceived on the biological plane and my consciousness is just their passive witness:

> They resemble those which I may observe in my friend Peter when I meet him after a separation. These demands for reassurance were expressly satisfied by Bergson when he conceived his theory of the deeper Self, which endures and organizes itself, which is constantly contemporaneous with my consciousness of it and could not be overtaken by it, which is at the origin of our acts, not like a cataclysmic power, but in the same way as a father begets his children, so that the act, without proceeding out of the essence as a rigorous consequence, without even being foreseeable, keeps up with it a reassuring relationship, a family resemblance; it goes further but along the same road. It preserves, of course, a certain irreducibility, but we recognize ourselves in it as a father can recognize himself and learn about himself in the son who pursues his task. Thus, through a projection of the liberty which we feel in ourselves into a psychic object which is the Self, Bergson contributed to disguise our anguish, but at the expense of consciousness itself.[15]

Not satisfied with deriding a liberty which would only consist in the interpenetration of past and present, Sartre denies that it could be effective, even in a limited way. The past, as Bergson conceives it, immanent although not active, is only a sort of household god with an honorary existence. It is a present "in retirement." Bergson, indeed, partly grounds his demonstration of liberty on his distinction between what is accomplished and what is being accomplished, between the become and the becoming, but his fault, which was that of Descartes, was to fail to recognize the nihilating character of consciousness: "The past thus may well be conceived as being *within* the present, but one has deprived oneself of the means to present this immanence otherwise than that of a stone at the bottom of a river." [16]

This is a severe criticism and we shall come back to it; we must first oppose to the Bergsonian conception of duration the Sartrean conception of temporality:

> Temporality is obviously an organized structure and these three so-called "elements" of time: past, present, future, must not be envisaged as a collection of "data" to be added—for instance as an indefinite series of "nows" some of which are not yet, some of which are no more—but as structural moments of an original synthesis. Otherwise we shall immediately encounter this paradox: the past is no more, the future is not yet, as to the instantaneous present, every one knows that it is not at all; it is the limit of infinite division, like the undivided point. [17]

Now, for Sartre, the past is not a nothingness, but it exists in function of the present and of the future, "tied up" to a certain present and to a certain future; it is characterized as "the past *of* something or *of* somebody." It exists "for us." The relations of the past to the present are those of the in-itself to the for-itself:

> If then I *am* not my own past, it cannot be on the original mode of becoming, but in so far as I *have to be it* in order *not to be it* and that I *have not to be it in order to be it*. This must enlighten us on the nature of the mode "was"; if I am not what I was, it is not because I have changed, which would presuppose time as given, it is because I am in relation to my being on the mode of internal connection of *not being*. [18]

The past is, as Hegel proclaimed, what I truly am, or, as Sartre prefers to call it: "the in-itself I am inasmuch as I am past it." [19]

As to the present, the ideal term of a division carried to infinity, it is merely *presence* of the for-itself to the in-itself, to the whole in-itself, i. e., to the world which it synthesizes; or rather, it is the presence of consciousness which makes a totality out of the world of things. However:

> Presence to a being implies that one is connected with a being by a bond of interiority . . . but this bond of interiority is a subjective bond, it denies of the present being that it is the being to which it is present. [20]

To that extent, one can say that the present *is not*. It simply makes itself present to a being in order to run away towards a future being.

Thus the phantom of non-being, bestriding the solid positive reality to which it is attached, is capable, not only of objectifying itself but also of tearing itself away from that reality as future presence to a being not yet in existence, precisely because it lacks being. Finality, in this system, functions as a sort of causality in reverse. The end explains the means, and the position I rapidly take on the tennis-court can only be explained by the gesture I shall take later to send back the ball over the net.

The whole structure of temporality is therefore a dispersion and a succession characterized by irreversibility. It is irreversible because the for-itself is necessarily a flight away from the in-itself. One sees how Bergsonian duration may seem inarticulate to Sartre:

> . . . Bergson, with his duration which is a melodic organization and a multiplicity of interpenetration does not seem to see that an organization of multiplicity presupposes an organizing act. . . . This Bergsonian past, which adheres to the present and even penetrates it, is hardly anything more than a rhetorical figure. And this is well demonstrated by the difficulties which Bergson encountered in his theory on memory. For if the Past, as he affirms, is the non-acting, it can only stay behind, it will never come back to

penetrate the present under the form of a memory, unless a present being has assumed the task of existing ek-statically in the Past.[21]

It seems that an abyss separates these two conceptions of the connections between time and liberty. Is it as deep as it first appears? Let us first take note of what they seem to have in common. Sartre's distinction between being-in-itself and being-for-itself immediately calls to mind Bergson's distinction between the become and the becoming: on one side a constant effort of the for-itself to free itself from the in-itself, on the other the continuous inventiveness of life striving to free itself from the automatism into which it is always about to stray; obviously Sartre is right to state that Bergson's thought moves on the biological plane. Is he right in considering the Bergsonian act as the product pure and simple of a fully constituted past? The author of *Creative Evolution* certainly does not grant any less to finality than the author of *Being and Nothingness,* and the *vis a posteriori* which Bergson opposes to the *vis a tergo* is nothing else than Sartre's causality in reverse. With Bergson, these two forces are fused in the indivisible movement of the act; to the extent that, with Sartre, there is no liberty except as a reaction to a given situation, and no future except in relation to a given past, the two philosophies are not without similarity. Does not Sartre seek in the act the efficacy of liberty which he does not find in being? No doubt the Bergsonian theory grants more to the past, but does not that past involve an initial project and an organizing act *sui generis?* Granting again that this organizing act, the *élan vital,* is conceived on the biological plane, does it not correspond to man's fundamental project according to Sartre: grounding being in liberty?

With Bergson, as to a certain extent with Sartre, the effort of the acting being bears on the present, but the present is defined as "the extension of the field which our attention to life can encompass," [22] and in this contact with the things of the material world, distinct and juxtaposed as they are, the mind must adopt its characters since it makes itself conscious of them. Thus arises the instant, which is not an ek-static position of consciousness in relation to being, but a mere projection within the idea of duration of an empirical spatial datum which is the point. It is therefore at the periphery of consciousness, so to speak, that one finds, as a "solidified crust," the symbolic concepts borrowed from the world of matter on which the mind wants to act. As introspection plunges deeper into the Self, it finds there, purer and purer, a "continuous flow": the still living past which one carries with him. It is not placed "in retirement" but rather into a reserve from which some unknown event may call it back through total mobilization of the being's forces: "An attention to life which would be sufficiently powerful and sufficiently freed from any practical interest, would therefore embrace in an undivided present the whole past history of the person. . . ." [23] This theory, which, on the aesthetic plane, presided over the conception of *Remembrance of Things Past,* also explains certain mystical states. It is also near to what Sartre calls "purified ecstasy," the complete detachment from the past which allows us to see it with full lucidity, before we adopt a new view of life. We must note, however, that Bergson's "attention to life" is ambiguous. Sometimes, as here, it refers to a complete adherence of consciousness to life; sometimes, it is, paradoxically, a sort of blacking-out process by which consciousness ignores whatever is not of immediate concern to its present preoccupations. Thus the drowning man who lives his whole past life in the flash of an instant does so, not through attention to life but through inattention born out of a feeling of helplessness.

Bergson, it would seem, implicitly recognizes the nihilating power of consciousness when he defines it as the faculty by which we are able to ignore any experience irrelevant to action, but he shows no awareness of the "split of being" around which the Sartrean definition of temporality revolves. To Bergson, there is no break in the life of the "deeper Self": "It is a succession of states each one of which announces that which follows and contains that which precedes." [24] Consciousness adheres to life, is contemporaneous with it, and it is only when I turn back to reflect on what happened to me that the reflective mind makes me detect multiple and distinct states of consciousness: "As long as I experienced them they were so solidly organized, so deeply animated by a common life, that I could not have told where any one of them ends, where the other begins." [25] If I can conceive of my successive states of mind as distinct from each other, it is through some faulty operation of the mind which makes me project into psychic continuity the reciprocal exteriority of things.

Sartre disclaims, as much as Bergson does, that mechanistic psychology which makes us consider our states of mind as psychic entities, acting as autonomous forces within our consciousness: a memory, let us say, which brings about jealousy, which precipitates an act of violence; this form of thinking he defines as bad faith on the plane of impure reflection; but, according to him, impure reflection would not be possible if reflection itself did not constitute in some way a certain manner of being oneself without being oneself, a certain way of being *for* oneself, a *presence* to self. It is in this dissociation, not in the continuity of our psychic life, that Sartre detects the source of liberty.

We have reached an irreducible divergence of viewpoints, and it is of the same nature as that which we have observed between the Sartrean and the Bergsonian definitions of non-being; or, more exactly, it is the same divergence, which comes from the fact that the two philosophies have their starting point and develop on two different planes. Bergson starts from the plane of doing in order to reach being (or rather becoming, perhaps to refrain from crossing the threshold which might lead him into pure mysticism); Sartre, on the contrary, starts with the quest of being (but is not this being which contains non-being in its core like a worm already a synthesis of being and non-being?) to end in a philosophy of *doing*. We shall find the same difference of orientation on the plane of man's relations with others, and on the plane of man's relations with the cosmos.

The social being is not, according to Sartre, distinct from the thinking being discovered by the Cartesian *cogito;* it implies that being. In the same ways as I affirm my existence on the background of the material world, I affirm my existence as distinct from that of the other by denying that I am the other; but that negation is of a different character in so far as it is an internal negation. The other is another Self, my *alter Ego*. He is "innermost in myself . . . as not being myself." The multiplicity of consciousnesses must constitute, as Hegel claims, a *totality* rather than a *collection,* and yet that totality is such that it is by principle impossible for me to adopt the point of view of the Whole, since I cannot affirm my Self except by denying that I am the other:

> Everything happens as if my ipseity facing that of others was produced and maintained in being by a totality which would carry to the extreme its own nihilation. . . . In this sense everything happens as if the others and myself were marking the vain effort of a totality of for-itself to recapture itself and to encompass what it *has to be* in the pure and simple mode of the-in-itself.[26]

Being-for-others constitutes the third attempt of being to tear itself away from contingency. The first is that by which being becomes for-itself; the second is that by which consciousness becomes self-consciousness, or reflective consciousness. But this stage is transitional; "the reflective ek-stasy finds itself on the way to a more radical ek-stasy: being for others."[27] Unable to ground its foundation in its own transparency, consciousness seeks it in the consciousness of others. According to Sartre, however, if the other grants me recognition, it is as an *object* for his consciousness, as a sort of being-in-itself immersed in the flux of life, and whose possibilities have become probabilities. If I reverse the process and affirm my subjectivity, the other becomes an object for my consciousness and I can no longer seek my justification in his. We are dealing here with an experience daily illustrated in the encounter of human glances. It is only on the plane of doing that we can experience, laterally so to speak, the subjectivity of others, as we all tend towards a common object. In spite of Sartre's allusion to an original totality of consciousness, which seems to be part of our individual consciousness, conflict is the basis of my relations with others on the plane of being. Collective solidarity is on the basis of common action and retains an accidental character. How does Bergson envisage the relation of one consciousness with another?

Sartre remarks that: "In a philosophy based on intuition, there is no intuition of the soul of others." [28] It is true that intuition figures, most of the time, in Bergson as the fringe of instinct and that the conception of liberty as expressing organized duration allows little room for the intuition of the other's Self. This duration is a form of the *élan vital,* and the conflicts involved, or entailed, by this single surge of life are purely contingent. There is indeed room for intuition on the vital plane, if not on that of individual consciousness, and it is that intuition which Bergson, in the last stage of his philosophy, hoped to see evolve into "a diffused mystical intuition." Thus, with Bergson, it is conflict which is accidental, as the result of individual variations within a single vital surge. One might object that conflict, whichever way one looks at it, implies some sort of separation; the animal which knows exactly where to strike its foe to kill or paralyze it, may act through intuitive knowledge of life's processes, but must operate a distinction *sui generis* between his life and the life of the other animal. Thus, one might well wonder whether Bergson does not implicitly recognize, on the plane of life and within the very process of intuition, that separation between beings which Sartre considers as the result of human consciousness. It is difficult to conceive the lion-to-gazelle relation as one of pure intuitive love, a struggle for life devoid of a crude biological sense of separateness.

As to the relations between individual consciousness and collective consciousness, they appear, as we know, in Bergson, under the form of a dialectical process rather than that of a conflict. While hardly granting more than a negative role to collective consciousness, Bergson recognizes its existence as such; it is collective consciousness which, at first opposing the innovations of individual initiative, finally adapts these innovations to its needs and preserves them under that modified form. From the rhythm of that dialectical process, progress is born. The collective soul, a product of the preservation instinct of closed communities, only aims at maintaining the integrity of the group; the effort of individual expansion, on the contrary, having its source in the very depth of the *élan vital,* could not, in its purer form, aim at anything else than the welfare of humanity as a whole. It is clear that, for Bergson, human liberty, when it is not contaminated by the selfish calculations of intelligence, may be resolved into a unique movement of biological and spiritual ascension, while for Sartre it is a matter of a "detotalized totality" of consciousness, which renders the "scandal of plurality of consciousnesses" irreparable. We cannot, therefore, pursue our parallel any further on that point. It is strange that after such a marked divergence on the social plane the two philosophies should seem to meet for a while on that of man's relation with the world of things.

6. "HOMO FABER" AND THE UTENSIL-WORLD

By this mere expression: the utensility of the world, Sartre sums up a whole side of Bergsonian philosophy, that which defines our conception of the external world as the scheme of all the possible activities offered to our industry, as a tissue in which it delineates the ideal lines of imaginary patterns. This notion of utensility Sartre extends to all that constitutes our world, starting from the center of reference offered by our consciousness acting through our body. Whether this conception is borrowed from Bergson or from Heidegger, Sartre seems to agree with Bergson on this point. The world's instrumentality, however, assumes a distinct character in the two philosophies.

Bergson sees in it a particular trend taken by creative evolution, a specific answer to the need for liberty adopted, in man's case, by the *élan vital,* and consisting merely in acting through inorganic, rather than through organic, matter. In the very domain of fabrication, we stray little from biological necessities: man *makes* the instrument which the animal *grows.* Sartre sees in "doing" or "making" merely a category of "being": fundamentally, we make objects in order to *have* them, i.e. so that they may represent symbolically a sort of extension of our *being.* Our possessions are, in a way, part of ourselves, since they are *for* us, and since we can wear them out or destroy them; and yet they are distinct from us, and to that extent they have *in themselves* an existence of their own. What is true of *making* is true of *doing,* even when our actions seem disinterested, as in art, politics, learning, or even sport; for in art we seek to create objects which, being us, still have a life distinct from ours; in politics, the "haves" defend the world which they have made theirs against the revolutionists who would like to change it into a world which would owe them its origin. Learning aims at the acquisition of knowledge, and indulging in sports is living in a world the laws of which we have made or accepted. Thus, through the world, man still seeks to do away with his contingency and to ground his being in consciousness. In the very knowledge of that contingency, of his psyche, of the situation where he finds himself, it is his own being that he is trying to appropriate, to place on a free basis; and it is in the individual consciousness, not on the biological plane of universal becoming, that Sartre envisages the relations of man with his world.

There is for Sartre no liberty without an aim, and no gratuitous act. All individual projects are only varied forms of a single original human project which is the realization of Being-in-itself-for-itself. This Being-in-itself-for-itself, grounded in its own consciousness and cause of itself corresponds to the definition of God. Sartre concludes that the aim of liberty is God's existence, or that man is a being who wants to be God. On all planes, and in every form, Sartre tries to demonstrate that this project involves a contradiction which makes failure inevitable. Human reality is a passion in the sense that "it projects to lose itself in order to ground Being and to constitute at the same time the In-itself which escapes contingency by being its own foundation . . . man loses himself so that God may be born," but he loses himself in vain: "man is a useless passion." [29]

To that conclusion, we may compare that of *The Two Sources of Morality and Religion,* a work which represents the last stage of Bergsonian thought:

> Humanity moans, half crushed by the weight of the progresses it has made. It is not sufficiently aware that its future depends upon itself. It is up to Humanity to see first whether it merely wants to live, or to supply also the necessary effort so that even on our refractory planet may be accomplished the essential function of the universe which is a machine to make Gods.[30]

The similarity between the conclusions of two conflicting philosophies of liberty ought not to surprise us. The ultimate end of liberty, after triumphing over external necessity, could be no other than ridding itself of its original contingency, becoming its own cause, identifying itself with the idea of God, or losing itself in that effort. In Bergson's thought, however, the concept of God may apply either to the protecting divinity of the City or to the creative force perceived by individual intuition; the closing paragraph of *The Two Sources* clearly indicates that we are deal-

ing with the latter under the form of "diffused mystical intuition." Sartre would hardly contemplate the possibility of this
diffusion on a universal plane, or as a function of the universe.
The fact remains that, with both philosophers, the idea of God
is an absolute value which calls for its realization in the future:
the end rather than the beginning of all things.

Starting from the quest of being, Sartre ends with a philosophy of action, and sees no effective realization of liberty except in "commitment." Through commitment, man will henceforward know that he is always able to define his essence and,
to that extent, master his destiny. Starting with an activistic philosophy, Bergson sees in the apparent discontinuity of the mind
only a reflection of the discontinuity of things, and never ceases
to postulate, through the forms assumed by creative evolution,
the immanence of a unique vital and spiritual impulse. Since, to
a certain degree, we *are* that impulse, and have access to it
through intuition, one may say that this activistic philosophy aims
at a direct and semi-mystical apprehension of Being.

We are mainly concerned here with two theories of liberty.
We can now see at a glance where they coincide and how they
differ.

Both Bergson and Sartre agree that there is no knowledge
except intuitive knowledge. Both strive to reduce knowing to
being; Bergson calls this knowledge *intuition,* and defines it as
the attention that the mind gives to itself while it is fixed upon
matter, its object. Sartre calls it "being-for-itself." Both define
our conception of the world as primarily a tool-complex. Both
stress finality as a universal project, which Bergson extends to
life, while Sartre reserves it to human consciousness. Furthermore, while rejecting the concepts of negation and of non-being
as pseudo-ideas, Bergson, like Heidegger and Sartre, implicitly
recognizes that the primary function of consciousness is to draw
a veil over being and withdraw that veil at its convenience, and
this conception of consciousness leads him to consider the primary

function of memory as that of forgetting, so to speak, what we do not need to remember. Such similarities can hardly be fortuitous and suggest the fact that, directly or indirectly, Sartre's philosophy of existence rests in part on Bergson's philosophy of life. In absolute opposition with Bergson, Sartre nevertheless continues his work by placing at the core of intuition the phantom of non-being that Bergson had so summarily dismissed.

Defining intuition as "the attention that the mind gives to itself, over and above, while it is fixed upon matter, its object," Bergson had suggested that it could be made the subject of further analysis: "This supplementary attention can be methodically cultivated and developed. Thus will be constituted a science of the mind, a veritable metaphysics which will define the mind positively instead of simply denying, concerning it, all that we know about matter." [31] This is precisely what Sartre did in his "phenomenological ontology," but not strictly along the lines prescribed, since, with him, "the attention the mind gives to itself" turns out to be a mere identity denied, a negation borne on the non-being which is presumably dwelling within the heart of the more elementary awareness.

And we must admit that, so long as we concentrate our attention on the structure of consciousness, Sartre's conception of a being-for-itself which always negates its identity with its object, even when it *is* its own object, is far more satisfactory than that of an "intuition" which would coincide exactly with its object. We are pleased, no doubt, with the notion that the knower can, through "intuition," identify himself with the known, which at least does away with the irritating question of what knowledge is. Still, we do not understand how, in the single act of intuition, the knower can distinguish himself from the known without some sort of split within his being, which, of course, renders impossible any form of complete identification. Sartre's theory throws light on the distinction between the knowing self and the known self; he also reduces knowing to being, but to a modified form of being which is being-for-itself. Being for ourselves adds—literally—nothing to our being, and the modification is only in the negative act by which we negate being what we are. Bestriding the solid positive reality to which it is attached, the phantom does exist in its own way, since it modifies the solid reality to which it is attached; it becomes from then on a familiar presence in all the structures of Sartre's astonishing "science of the mind."

One may wonder wherefrom the phantom draws its paradoxical existence. This is a metaphysical question which Sartre raises but does not care to answer. His philosophy of existence does not call for hypothetical explanations of what lies beyond the structures of human consciousness. At this point, we would welcome the wider perspectives of a philosophy of life which, like Bergson's, would allow us a glimpse at the progressive disentanglement of Mind from Matter, of liberty from necessity; but just as Bergson's philosophy of life fails to give a plausible account of the transition from life to consciousness, so does Sartre's philosophy of existence fail to retrace to some sort of biological evolution the sudden irruption of non-being into being which, according to him, human consciousness represents.

We understand, from a private conversation with M. Sartre, that he is in no way unaware of the problem involved; that he conceives the possibility that human consciousness may be the last stage of a long disaggregation of being on the biological plane; but, just as Bergson's philosophy of life could not account for man's consciousness without surrendering its position on the plane of creative evolution, Sartre's philosophy of existence could not abandon its position on the plane of human consciousness without betraying its method and its fundamental assumption.

8. LIFE AND EXISTENCE

Neither Bergson nor Sartre claims to have reached metaphysical conclusions. Bergson merely indicates the general direction toward which the teachings of natural sciences and of intuition seem to converge; Sartre is satisfied with opening for us a few metaphysical perspectives. Both prefer to remain on the safer ground of an "as if" philosophy aiming at the communication of an intuition rather than at a strict demonstration. Such a philosophy, depending as it does on the suggestive power of imagery, has definite affinities with literature. It is then no wonder if Bergson's philosophy assumes a literary character as it reaches its conclusion in the form of cosmic visions.

Schelling's notion of *Identität,* identity of God, man, and the cosmos, had penetrated the French idealist tradition somewhat altered by Ravaisson's suggestion that physical laws were, so to speak, mere habits, a routine engendered by the cooling-off process of creation. Bergson had made excellent use of this notion, but his philosophy of creative evolution still managed to preserve a kind of continuity among all parts of creation:

> Let us imagine a vessel full of steam at a high pressure, and here and there in its side a crack through which the steam is escaping in a jet. The steam thrown into the air is nearly all condensed into little drops which fall back, and this condensation and this fall represent simply the loss of something, an interruption, a deficit. But a small part of the jet of steam subsists, uncondensed, for some seconds; it is making an effort to raise the drops which are falling; it succeeds at most in retarding their fall. So, from an immense reservoir of life, jets must be gushing out unceasingly, of which each, falling back, is a world.[32]

The philosophy of creative evolution, in last analysis, was still based on a romantic belief in the identity of man's mind with life's creative force, the *élan vital.* No doubt this identity was dimmed by the tendency of *homo faber,* man the artisan, to see the world as a complex of tools, and therefore to think of life in terms of inorganic matter, but the original impulse of creation could somehow be retrieved through intuition, and the world could still evolve toward a sort of diffused mysticism.

As the smallest grain of dust is bound up with our entire solar system, drawn along with it in that undivided movement of descent which is materiality itself, so all organized beings, from the humblest to the highest, from the first origins of life to the time in which we are, and in all places as in all times, do but evidence a single impulsion, the inverse of the movement of matter, and in itself indivisible. All the living hold together, and all yield to the same tremendous push. The animal takes its stand on the plant, man bestrides animality, and the whole of humanity, in space and in time, is one immense army galloping beside and before and behind each of us in an overwhelming charge able to beat down every resistance and clear the most formidable obstacles, perhaps even death.[33]

If Bergson's philosophy had turned to literary expression in order to communicate these cosmic visions, Sartre, in his first novel, uses philosophical literature to dispel them.

To Sartre as to Heidegger, consciousness is primarily a separation from the flow of life, an *ek-stasy*. In fact, to Sartre, knowledge is *identity denied*. Sartre, then, marks the most definite break between the philosophy of life and the philosophy of existence. This does not mean that Sartre rejects all the elements of the philosophy of life; but what he retains is brought down from the plane of biology to the plane of individual consciousness, with the separation implied by the reflective process.

This fundamental separation, it seems to me, is most clearly illustrated in *Nausea*. To the hero, Roquentin, the world suddenly has ceased to be a complex of tools:

Objects, they ought not to *touch* you, since they don't live. You use them, put them back into their place, live among them; they are useful, nothing more. And they touch me, it's unbearable; I am afraid to enter into contact with them; it is as if they were living beasts.[34]

It all started as Roquentin was holding a pebble that he had picked up on the beach: "Now I see; I remember better what I felt the other day, by the sea, holding that pebble. It was a sort of sweetish, nauseating sensation. How unpleasant it was!"[35] This nausea is a first premonition of the absurd contingency of things as they are in themselves. The full discovery occurs in the famous episode of the root of the chestnut tree:

> Absurdity was not an idea in my head, nor a mere articulated breath, but this long serpent at my feet, this wooden serpent; serpent, claw, root, or vulture's talon, it matters little. And without formulating anything else clearly, I distinctly understood that I had found the key to my Nausea, to my own life.[36]

Before the reality of the root, viewed in itself, outside of its function, outside of the very stubbornness of life which it conveyed, one single intuition stood out: the absurdity of its contingency. The root simply was there; any explanation for its essence or for its nature came as an afterthought. As this strange fascination subsides, when Roquentin is at last able to look away from the root, he experiences a feeling of complete emptiness—the non-being in his own consciousness—after which he sees the swaying foliage in the background. For a moment, he believes that he is going to detect the dynamic forces of nature at work: "to see existences being born," but he soon gives up this illusion; life does not know itself in these swaying trees, each one of its moments is full and compact, there is no *élan vital;* the surge toward the future is purely human: the trees simply persist in being. Yet, before leaving the scene, Roquentin feels as if the whole park were smiling at him:

> Things were like thoughts which stopped half-way, forgot themselves, forgot what they had wanted to think and remained just so, dangling, with an odd little meaning which went beyond them. It annoyed me, that little meaning: I could not understand it, even if I had remained one hundred and seven years against that gate; I had learned about existence all I could know.[37]

A whole book has been written to prove that, by ignoring the "odd little meaning," Sartre, through Roquentin, was turning his back to creation and to God. Let us simply conclude that he was turning his back to the philosophy of life and creative evolution which started with romantic nature mysticism. When he wrote *Nausea* at Le Hâvre, where he was teaching philosophy, Sartre was still struggling to free himself from the obsession of living forms, imprisoned, so to speak, in the hard shell of their realization. Not only did he imagine, as he looked at the sea, the possible emergence of some huge crab, as wide as an island, not only did this obsession take the form of an hallucination that crustaceans were following him, but all the inhabitants of Le Hâvre, the good citizens going through their customary courtesies as they met coming out of church, the ship builders and other respectable persons whose portraits covered the walls of a gallery reserved to outstanding citizens, even the poor self-taught humanist who thought that he could absorb all knowledge by reading the books of the library in alphabetical order, appeared to him as the grotesque puppets of a Kafkaësque world. Only music, or literature, could free him from this morass.

To Sartre, as to Pascal before him, if custom is a second nature it might be that nature itself is only custom, i.e., repetition, inertia, and somnolence. At this point, the romantic tradition, as modified by Ravaisson and Bergson, seems to meet with the humanistic tradition represented by Pascal. But this meeting is partly an illusion. Pascal's intuition simply situates *fallen man within a fallen world,* while Bergson shows life triumphant through all its defeats, in the single impulsion of creative evolution, and manages to preserve a sort of continuity between living species. To Sartre, human consciousness marks the irruption of non-being into being and the triumph of discontinuity. Paradoxically, Sartre is closer, in some ways, to Pascal than to Bergson, and his existentialism is indeed, as he claims, a form of humanism.

3

Existentialism and Humanism

Self-love is love of self and of all things
for itself.

Self-love only wants to be.

LA ROCHEFOUCAULD, *Maxims*

I. HUMANISM, CLASSICAL AND MODERN

L'Existentialisme est un humanisme: such is the title
of the only popular treatise written by Sartre. Being the text of
a lecture followed by a debate between the author and a Marxist,
this essay appears at first to be an attack on dialectical materialism, but it also contains criticism of the "intelligible heaven" of
idealism. Pure materialism and pure idealism are indeed considered by the humanist as dehumanizing disciplines. In pure
materialism, man becomes part of a machinery lost in universal
determinism; in pure idealism, he loses his identity in divine
subjectivity. Modern vitalism, in which the person is immersed
in the flux of life, or becomes part of the vital impetus, fares no
better with the humanist.

Any form of humanism implies belief in something absolute
and immanent within man which is generally referred to as
"human nature." Sixteenth- and seventeenth-century humanism
sought that permanent element in the fact that man had been
created in the image of God. When the French "moralists" of

the Classical Age speak of Man, they think of him as being outside of time and space, like God, some of whose attributes classical
Man seems to have inherited from the theocentric Middle Ages;
or if they do think of man as situated in time and space, it is
still with some of the attributes of infinity.

In the eighteenth century, humanism is pulled apart by
two divergent forces: on the one hand, Cartesian belief in "innate ideas" is shaken by Locke's sensationalism, which is to
lead to nineteenth-century positivism and naturalism; on the
other hand, a recrudescence of mysticism of a quietist, pantheistic,
or esoteric character has already started the movement which is
to lead to romanticism and symbolism. The alternate triumphs
of these two trends were equally unfavorable to the humanistic
attitude.

Not until the twentieth century were various attempts made
to formulate, on a non-religious basis, a new form of humanism.
This neo-humanism in France, Germany, and America took
first of all the form of an attack on the romantic heritage represented by various irrational forces; but the religious postulates
of seventeenth-century humanism could not be so easily replaced
by the social consciousness implied by Irving Babbitt's "inner
check," nor by Ernest Seillière's warnings against "naturistic
mysticism," nor by Thomas Mann's plea for a reconciliation of
the Apollonian with the Faustian outlooks. We need hardly dwell
on the humanism of Anatole France and Romain Rolland. In
spite of their personal commitment to human values, these two
authors took a somewhat too detached attitude for the temper of
the age. France's elegant skepticism tinged with irony and pity
remained that of a spectator of human affairs, provided mostly
negative values, and soon made of him a living anachronism.
Romain Rolland's humanism, more positive, progressive, and
universal, did provide a metaphysical value, the presence in all
men of a God that lives and suffers with them; but either because this doctrine was too close to mysticism or because his con-

temporaries resented Rolland's claim to the right of standing "above the battle" in World War I, his philosophy failed to provide the basis for a new humanism. Neo-romanticism continued to thrive under the guise of Bergsonism and surrealism, while its foe-brother, naturalism, reached unprecedented popularity.

Around 1930, the idea was born in a few eager and anguished minds that the basic image of Man which had been sought in and outside religion was no longer to be rediscovered, but created in action, through his own flesh, by the writer himself. Thus arose the idea of a literature of commitment which would merely be, as it were, the orchestration of the author's existence. Camus provided the notion of man as a stranger to the absurdity of his own existence. Saint Exupéry showed the new leader unifying the world through his action, forcing men to transcend their transitory existence through their work, creating a new image of man through his own personal triumph over fear and death. But it was Malraux who gave the most complete formula for a new, tragic, and universal type of humanism. In him one finds the rare fusion of the man of action with the intellectual. His humanism has roots in the tradition of French humanism, in Montaigne, in Pascal; but it expands through his studies of past and exotic cultures into a sort of universal humanism. Moreover, it points to a form of humanism, the values of which are no longer in the past but in the future. Not only is God dead, as Nietzsche had proclaimed, but so is Man. As man discovers himself in extreme situations, he defines humanity anew. Thus Katow, in *La Condition humaine,* when he walks toward the locomotive in which he is to be burned alive, after giving away to weaker prison mates the poison pellets which could have spared him a horrible death, evokes in the mind of the other prisoners an image of man greater than his condition.

Jean-Paul Sartre's distinction was to endow the literature of commitment with a philosophy, and to establish the connection between this movement, and the new trends of phenomenology and existentialism. The Germanic sources of existentialism being well established, the aim of this essay is to find out how Sartrean existentialism fits into, or departs from, the main current of French humanism. The connections might be found to be somewhat closer than one might have expected, for French humanism and existentialism have at least one source in common, which is the Augustinian tradition.

2. THE AUGUSTINIAN IMAGE OF MAN

The Augustinian trend which started in French humanism with the rejection of scholasticism at the dawn of the Renaissance is an undeniable, even though imperfectly recognized, fact. Augustine's *"Dilige et quod vis fac,"* "Love and do what thou wilt," receives a distant echo in Rabelais' "Do what thou wilt," and in his definition of faith as "formed from charity"; Calvin's doctrine of grace is, of course, directly borrowed from Augustine, as well as Luther's doctrine of God's immanence in man. Montaigne, it is true, widened the scope of French humanism and brought it closer to classical sources, but in the following century his skepticism was eagerly seized upon and reinterpreted in the light of Augustianism by Descartes and Pascal.

It is a well-known fact that Descartes' *cogito* has its source, probably indirectly, in Augustine's *"Si fallor, sum,"* "If I deceive myself, I am," and also in the following dialogue: "R. You who wish to understand yourself, do you know that you exist?—A. I know it.—R. How do you know it?—A. I know not.—R. Do you know that you are thinking?—A. I do.—R. Therefore it is true that you think?—A. True." [1] To quote Gilson:

> . . . like Descartes, he had issued from his doubt, thanks to the triumphant evidence of his "si fallor sum"; like Descartes, finally, he had from the evidence of thought, held by direct grasp, drawn the certitude of the spirituality and immortality of the soul, as well as the proof of the existence of God. [2]

The resemblance is more apparent than real. Augustine starts with doubt, it is true, but his doubt is not a matter of method, it is an immediate and anguishing experience: *Irrequietum est cor nostrum:* "Restless is our heart." Descartes' method is to apply to philosophy the clear and distinct ideas which he found useful in mathematics, while Augustine finds it essential to start with an act of faith resulting in the mystical vision generally referred to as the Augustinian illumination, and comparable to the *esprit de finesse,* or intuitive mind which Pascal opposes to the mathematical mind. The Augustinian illumination, like the intuitive mind, described by Pascal as an attempt "to see the matter at once, at one glance, and not by a process of reasoning," is really only a starting point for a way of thinking which consists in trying to proceed from unity to multiplicity, from intuition to discursive thought. Furthermore, and above all, Descartes' *cogito* represents the effort of thought to get hold of its being, at least as thinking substance, the world having been left behind in the suspense of universal doubt. Augustine's *Si fallor, sum* finds him situated, as a thinking man, with a mind and a body, in a universe which comprises all degrees of reality: inorganic being which only is; the plant which is and lives; the animal which lives and feels; man who lives, feels, and thinks. Thought, therefore, apprehends itself as being at the top of that hierarchy and comprising the other degrees as inferior potentialities.

It may be said, then, that Augustine had anticipated Descartes' *cogito,* but that Augustine's *cogito* is an existential *cogito,* inseparable from the world, with the situation assigned by a body, as in Pascal or Marcel; but we may go further and state that Augustine had anticipated as well Sartre's "pre-reflective *cogito,*" i.e., the presence of thought to itself even when it is completely absorbed by its object. To Augustine, thought is inseparable from self-knowledge, but "it does not place itself before itself, so to speak, to consider itself, unless it thinks itself." [3] It often happens that, present to itself as it is, thought does not perceive itself. This unnoticed presence is like a memory which one possesses but does not happen to be thinking about.

Descartes proceeds from the notion of his being, as thinking substance, to the notion of perfection, which was already implicit in the imperfection of his doubt, and to the existence of God, implicit in the notion of perfection. In the same way, Augustine derives the idea of God from the necessity of truth, which could not proceed from the contingency of the thinking subject, and must proceed from God; and indeed, to the mystic there is no difference between Truth and God. Descartes, to use Pascal's words, needs Him to "give a fillip to set the world in motion; beyond this he has no further need of God." [4] Like all early medieval philosophers, Augustine is primarily interested in the image of God which the mind of man must in some way have preserved, no matter how deformed by sin, since man was created in the image of God. Again like early medieval philosophers, he will seek God as Trinity, and Trinity itself through the Neo-Platonic philosophy of emanation. To Augustine, therefore, *The One* of Plotinus, True and only Being of the universe, superessential Non-Being which is the source of all emanation, corresponds to the Father; *Intelligence,* Plato's world of Forms, or Ideas, corresponds to the Son; The *Soul* of the World, which organizes the world and produces individual souls, corresponds to the Holy Ghost. The individual soul, therefore, is placed between the world of the spirit and the world of organic matter, which is to it a constant subject of temptation. Thought, being closer to God in the hierarchy of living beings, must in some way reflect this order, and throw back on it the light of its reflection.

The image of Trinity is found in the depth of man's thought as Mind, Knowledge, and Love. The act of conceiving the truth is only an image of the conception of the Word by the Father. It is Thought, already present to itself (like Sartre's pre-reflective *cogito*), knowing itself and expressing itself through words.

What then of the relations between the soul and the body, and, we might add, the external world, which in Descartes takes the form of the dualism of two separate substances mysteriously joined? According to Augustine, the soul takes care of the body, and its relations to the body are made up of *attentions*. It is the act of attention which constitutes sensation, and the nature of this attention which constitutes pain or pleasure. "For it is not the body that has sensation, but the soul through the body, and it uses the latter as, so to speak, a messenger in order to form within itself what is announced from without." [5] This theory, so strikingly close to Bergson's notion of consciousness as "attention" to life, also reminds us of Husserl's conception of consciousness as empty and "intentional."

This psychology of "attentions" constitutes the main difference between Augustinianism and Thomism. A great many attempt have been made lately to prove that the two philosophies harmoniously complement each other. St. Thomas Aquinas, however, followed Aristotle in positing an active intellect which abstracted the datum of sense, and was a power reserved to man. As D'Arcy observes:

> . . . in Augustine's philosophy there is no sensible image to be spiritualized, because the image is a product of expression of the soul acting through the body. If this be so, the office of the active intellect would be a sinecure. The sensible has no drawbridge to cross, because sensation is a sentinel of the mind.[6]

Augustine's theory on this point strangely reminds us of Sartre's theory of imagination, which also abolishes the "sensible image" as an idol of psychologism. To Augustine, the only active feature the mind recognizes is the feature of truth which is, so to speak, the light of God. Therefore, whereas the Aristotelian active intellect of the Thomists produces truth, as the adequation of the idea to the thing, the Augustinian illumination produces truth directly and constitutes, as in Heidegger and Sartre a sort of "unveiling," i.e. letting things be as they are. "The reasoning soul yields or refuses assent to interior images by choice of will." [7] The choice depends on our will, which is "fully free when it does not serve our vices." [8]

As, in Plotinus, the individual soul is situated in the Chain of Life, between the world of the spirit and the world of matter, the Augustinian soul is situated between the City of God and the Earthly City. The City of God is also the world of Will and the world of Love, since fully free will springs from love of God, and it is up to us to choose between the Earthly City and the City of God, between "avaricious" love of self and the generous love of God, between "knowledge" and "wisdom." Love of God is wisdom and it is also the surrender of self. In this supreme exaltation of the will as a God-given illumination, we can detect the paradox of the doctrine of Grace; we can also detect, since God alone has real being, a distant image of the existentialist choice between "inauthentic" and "authentic" life, as well as the basic notion of a "generosity" based on will in Cartesian ethics.

Can we call Augustine a mystic? Without being absolutely precise on the origin of the soul, Augustine does not consider it as a part of God but as created by God. At once immanent and transcendent, Augustine's God is indeed the absolute *Thou* of Christian existentialists. Yet there is no doubt that, in Augustine, the Neo-Platonic notion of participation predominates over the Aristotelian, or Thomistic, notion of efficient causality, which brings him closer to modern vitalistic thinking.

We found in Augustine therefore a forerunner of vitalistic thinking closely connected with the romantic tradition, as well as an image of man based on the dogma of the Trinity interpreted through Neo-Platonic philosophy, which image is at the core of French classical humanism: man, created free and immortal, separated himself from God through pride even before temptation. He preferred himself to God; and love of self, the original sin, has become his *nature*. Left to himself, man can only do evil since his very will is no longer pure will but perverted will. There are in man vestiges of his first nature which can become active through faith: but faith can only come from God.

A certain ambiguity in the definition of man's nature and of Grace has allowed various interpretations and heated controversies. What we cannot help retaining from it is a conception which makes of existence itself a sin, insofar as it is centered around the self. Before we reach the pure existentialist version of this notion in Sartre, we must now see how it fits in with the image of man which French Classicism has left us.

2. THE IMAGE OF MAN IN FRENCH CLASSICISM

It is really with Montaigne that the concept of a human *nature,* to be defined by the reflection of the image of God, is replaced by the concept of a universal human *condition,* which each man bears entirely and can discover by himself. By realizing, and accepting, the contingency and limitations of the human condition, concludes Montaigne at the end of his *Essays,* one may come to enjoy it as if it were an absolute: "It is an *absolute* perfection, and as it were *divine* for a man to know how to enjoy *his being* loyally." [9] Montaigne accepts his contingent being as Camus accepts his absurd being. Man again becomes with him the measure of all things: "The greatnesse of the minde is not so much, to drawe up and hale forward, as to know how to range, direct and circumscribe itselfe." [10] Centered around the discovery of man's estate, a new kind of literature is born, which consists in a series of digressions.

Pascal resumes these digressions and tries to make them converge on the thought of the hidden God, the *Deus absconditus,* which alone can give them meaning. To the extent that the spirit of man is unenlightened and dormant, the spell of literature must be used till, by the sudden light of truth, it may be awakened again, through a process akin to poetical evocation.

The first existential theme we encounter in Pascal is the realization of man's situation between the two infinites of magnitude and of smallness. While Pascal's cosmogony is indeed more a poetical vision than a scientific hypothesis, the whole passage somehow manages to evoke that awakening to a total situation which Heidegger calls *Gefindlichkeit.* In awe and wonder man finds himself situated in the center of things. Since he is indefinitely removed from comprehending the extremes, "the end of things and their beginning are hopelessly hidden from him in an impenetrable secret." [11] "Our intellect holds the same position in the world of thought as our body occupies in the expanse of nature." [12] As our senses perceive no extreme, in the same way, for our minds, extremes are as if they were not; yet we could not comprehend the part outside of the whole, the whole without the parts:

> This is our true state; this is what makes us incapable of certain knowledge and of absolute ignorance. We sail within a vast sphere, ever drifting in uncertainty, driven from end to end. When we think to attach ourselves to any point and to fasten to it, it wavers and leaves us; and we follow it, it eludes our grasp, slips past us and vanishes for ever. Nothing stays for us. This is our natural condition, and yet most contrary to our inclination; we burn with the desire to find solid ground and an ultimate sure foundation whereon to build a tower reaching to the infinite. But our whole groundwork cracks, and the earth opens to abysses.[13]

No one has expressed better than Pascal the feeling of *Contingency* which arises from the realization by consciousness of its situation in the Here and Now on the background of the whole universe:

> When I consider the short duration of my life, swallowed up in the eternity before and after, the little space which I fill, and even can see, engulfed in the infinite immensity of space of which I am ignorant, and which knows me not, I am frightened, and am astonished at being here rather than there; for there is no reason why here rather than there, why now rather than then.

The feeling of *Geworfenheit,* or *délaissement,* loosely translated as *Dereliction,* is not far off: "Who has put me here? By whose order and direction have this place and time been allowed to me?" [14] And *Anguish* follows closely: "The eternal silence of these infinite spaces frightens me." [15]

What completes our natural inability of knowing things is the fact that we are composed of soul and body and cannot perfectly know things that are simple, whether spiritual or corporal:

> Hence it comes that almost all philosophers have confused ideas of things and speak of material things in spiritual terms, and of spiritual things in material terms. For they say boldly that bodies have a tendency to fall, that they seek after their centre. . . .[16]

This notion, so basic to all existential thinking, from Kierkegaard to Sartre, is related to Sartre's objection to the theory of Marxism, that in Marxism "opposition" is sought in matter.

Reason, indeed, has been unable to define either the soul or the body or the relation between them. *Absurdity* rules the world through imagination and custom:

> He who would follow reason only would be deemed foolish by the generality of men. We must judge by the opinion of the majority of mankind. Because it has pleased them, we must work all day for pleasures seen to be imaginary; and after sleep has refreshed our tired reason, we must forthwise start up and rush after phantoms, and suffer the impressions of this mistress of the world.[17]

This mistress of the world, imagination, indeed rules over social existence: "We cannot even see an advocate in his robe and with his cap on his head, without a favourable opinion of his ability."[18] It always prevails over reason:

> If the greatest philosopher in the world find himself upon a plank wider than actually necessary, but hanging over a precipice, his imagination will prevail, though his reason convince him of his safety. Many cannot bear the thought without a cold sweat.[19]

It is interesting, at this point, to note that Montaigne, treating the same theme, is closer to Sartrean existentialism than Pascal:

Let a beame or planke be laid acrosse from one of those two steeples (of Notre Dame) to the other, as big, as thick, as strong, and as hard, as would suffice any man to walke safely upon it, there is no Philosophicall wisdom of so great resolution and constance that is able to encourage and perswade us to march upon it, as we would, were it below on the ground. I have sometimes made triall of it upon our mountains . . . and I could not without horror to my minde and trembling of leggs and thighes endure to looke on those infinite precipices and steepy downefals, though I were not neere the brim, nor any danger within my length and more; and *unlesse I had willingly gone to the perill,* I could not possibly have fallen.[20]

It is precisely, according to Sartre, the knowledge that nothing stands between me and the peril that causes me to realize in anguish my liberty grounded in nothingness.

To Sartre, imagination is intentional consciousness directed at an absent object and is therefore an expression of our freedom; so it is to Pascal, who sees in it a form of self-deceit:

Children who are frightened at the face they have blackened are but children. But how shall one who is so weak in his childhood become really strong when he grows older? We only change our fancies.[21]

This weakness by which we fall into self-deceit is compared by Sartre to the way in which we fall into sleep; to Pascal, who thinks that pure will could only come from God, it is the effect of the very perversion by which man's will has turned away from God and toward the self. We deceive ourselves when we think, as Montaigne does, that "Nature is a sweet guide" and that we can pattern our behavior after "natural principles."

What are our natural principles but principles of custom? In children they are those which they have received from the habits of their fathers, as hunting in animals. A different custom will cause different natural principles. . . .[22]

There is nothing that man may not make natural:

> Custom is a second nature which destroys the former. But what
> is nature? For is custom not natural? I am much afraid that nature
> is itself only a first custom, as custom is a second nature.[23]

Thus our beliefs in custom, or nature, are really the results of a
bias leading to error, the bias of a perverted and weakened will:

> The will, which prefers one aspect to another, turns away the
> mind from considering the qualities of all that it does not like
> to see. And thus the mind, moving in accord with the will, stops
> to consider the aspects which it likes, and so judges by what it
> sees.[24]

This is strictly according to Augustine's psychology of "attentions," Husserl's psychology of "intentions," and Sartrean psychoanalysis. The will, in Pascal, is deflected by self-love as, in Sartre,
toward the "individual project." But what is the nature of this
"self-love"?

> . . . the Self has two qualities: it is unjust in itself since *it makes
> itself the center of everything;* it is inconvenient to others since
> it would enslave them; for each self is the enemy, and would
> like to be the tyrant of all others. You take away its inconvenience,
> [by politeness] but not its injustice.[25]

As in Pascal, so in Sartre, the self is unjust in itself and inconvenient to others because it necessarily makes itself the center
of everything. It makes little difference that, on the plane of
action, this center becomes, with Sartre, an absolute center of
reference for a totalitarian organization of the world: what the
self wants is to persist in *being,* for itself and for others. Deprived
of the possibilities of action, Sartre's characters, in the Hell of
No Exit, try at first to do away with the "inconvenience" of the
situation through the complicity of politeness but cannot do away
with the fundamental "injustice" of each self. Hence it follows
that in Pascal, as later in Hegel and in Sartre, conflict is the basic
relation between one self and another; and yet one self cannot do
without the recognition of another:

We do not content ourselves with the life we have in ourselves and in our own being; we desire to live an imaginary life in the mind of others, and for this purpose we endeavour to shine. We labour unceasingly to adorn and preserve this imaginary existence, and neglect the real. . .

and it is indeed, as in Sartre, "a great proof of the nothingness of our being, not to be satisfied with the one without the other. . . ."[26]

It should be noted at this point that not in Pascal alone, but in all French writers under the influence of Jansenism, self-love is, if not the source of all our feelings, at least the misguiding force which directs their evolution. La Rochefoucauld's definition of self-love deserves a special mention as coming curiously close to Sartre's analysis of consciousness: "Self-love is the love of oneself and of everything else only *for oneself*. . . ."[27] It is already surprising to find the expression "for oneself" used in this connection by a seventeenth-century "moralist." Proceeding with La Rochefoucauld's definition, we find that self-love "is often invisible to itself," like Sartre's pre-reflective *cogito*:

But this thick miasma in which it hides from itself does not at all prevent it from observing the external world with perfect clarity, and in this it resembles our eyes which can see everything save only themselves.[28]

This self-love may fail to recognize its own designs:

. . . among its brood are some so monstrous that, when at last they are revealed by the light of day, their parent fails to recognize them or at least refuses to accept them as its progeny.[29]

No more in La Rochefoucauld than in Sartre, then, are these monstrous designs produced by some *libido* unknown to consciousness. Like Sartre, La Rochefoucauld considers passions as certain ways in which self-love prefers to manifest its liberty. After remarking how easily we sometimes get rid of them, he makes the statement that:

> . . . one may fairly deduce, with considerable probability, that its desires are the result of spontaneous combustion, rather than of the inflamation created by the beauty or value of the desired objects; that its own desire is the high price which it ascribes to their worth and the tinsel with which it embellishes their charm; that it is itself which it pursues, and that it is chasing its own liking when it chases that which is to its own liking.[30]

Self-love may turn to self-hatred or, as Sartre would express it, to the project of self-objectification, or masochism, and La Rochefoucauld's explanation of this paradox is basically the same as Sartre's:

> . . . it feeds on everything; and it feeds on nothing. . . . It will even be found among the ranks of those who are its declared foes. . . . And what is more remarkable is that, in their company, it will hate itself, it will plot its own overthrow, it will strive for its own ruination; for *it cares only that it should be, and so long as it continues to be* it is quite willing to do so as its own enemy.[31]

This self-love, which is as willing to "tyrannize over others" as to "hate itself" with them, could be moved neither by a Freudian *libido* nor by an Adlerian will-to-power. Its real nature is that of the Sartrean consciousness, or being-for-itself, which indeed easily passes from sadism to masochism because it feels its nothingness and, through power or suffering, merely seeks *being,* were it only for others. Sartre has little use for the moralists' "self-love"; commonly interpreted as meaning that our actions aim only at our own "interest," this notion no doubt deserves his contempt. Closely reconsidered, it reveals striking affinities with Heidegger's *Dasein* or Sartre's for-itself. We must note, however, that his "self-love," rooted as it is in Augustinianism, reveals the weakness of the will as well as its perversion.

A number of La Rochefoucauld's maxims treat of that weakness, sometimes under the head of laziness: "the most intense and malignant" of all our passions.[32] To all seventeenth-century humanists, weakness of the will is the clearest indication of man's fallen condition. The sentiment of our liberty, says Descartes, "renders us in some way similar to God, by making us the masters of ourselves, provided we do not lose, through cowardliness, the rights He gives us." [33] Sartre endorses with enthusiasm the first part of this statement, which is also implicit in the works of Saint Exupéry and Malraux. To Pascal, inasmuch as the will is depraved and turned toward the self it carries a certain automatism which brings man closer to Descartes' "animal-machine," and this is true even of the lust of will turned into a passion. For excellent reasons, Sartre could hardly accept such views, since to him laziness, or "softness," is a choice and a project, like any other way of being. Yet a distant echo of the Augustinian notion touching weakness of the will might be detected in his remark that "Every existent is born without reason, prolongs itself through weakness and dies by chance of encounter." [34] In this remark, as in the preceding quotations, we might perhaps make bold to detect a distant echo of the philosophy of emanation, which is one of the common sources of humanism and vitalism.

To sum up the picture of the limitations of the human condition as expressed by Pascal on the plane of contemplation:

> I know not who put me into the world, nor what the world is, nor what I myself am. I am in terrible ignorance of everything. I know not what my body is, nor my senses, nor my soul, not even that part of me which thinks what I say, which reflects on all and on itself, and knows itself no more than the rest. I see those frightful spaces of the universe which surround me, and I find myself tied to one corner of this vast expanse, without knowing why I am put in this place rather than in another, nor why the short time which is given to me is assigned to me at this point rather than at another of the whole eternity which was before me or which will come after me. I see nothing but infinity on all sides, which surrounds me as an atom and as a shadow which endures only for an instant and returns no more. All I know is that I must soon die, but what I know least is this very death which I cannot escape. [35]

As in Heidegger, man is conscious of the sea of non-being which surrounds his existence; he is also conscious of his *Sein zum Tode,* being for death. Pascal's final image of the human condition is the very conception which Malraux will illustrate and dramatize according to his own brand of humanism in his novel *La Condition humaine*, a title inaccurately rendered as *Man's Fate*. Here is Pascal's description:

> Let us imagine a number of men in chains, and all condemned to death, where some are killed each day in the sight of the others, and those who remain see their own fate in that of their fellows, and wait for their turn, looking at each other sorrowfully and without hope. It is an image of the condition of man.[36]

Facing the human condition, man, according to Heidegger, hesitates between assuming it or fleeing it in inauthentic life. This latter solution bears in Pascal the name of diversion:

> When I have occasionally set myself to consider the different distractions of men, the pains and perils to which they expose themselves at court or in war, whence arise so many quarrels, passions, bold and often bad ventures, etc., I have discovered that all the unhappiness of men arises from one single fact, that they cannot stay quietly in their own chamber. . . .
>
> But on further consideration, when after finding the cause of our ills, I have sought to discover the reason of it, I have found that there is one very real reason, namely the natural poverty of our feeble and mortal condition, so miserable that nothing can comfort us when we think of it closely.[37]

Hence the necessity of diversion; but there is no diversion without self-deceit:

> Hence it comes that play and the society of women, war and posts, are so sought after. Not that there is in fact any happiness in them, or that men imagine true bliss to consist in money won at play, or in the hare which they hunt; we would not take these as a gift. We do not seek that easy and peaceful lot which permits us to think of our unhappy condition, nor the dangers of war,

nor the labour of office, but the bustle which averts these thoughts of ours, and amuses us.[38]

Men will not face this fact; they like to think that when they have obtained what they are after they will be able to rest with pleasure:

> They have a secret instinct which impels them to seek amusement and occupation abroad, and which arises from the sense of their constant unhappiness. They have another secret instinct, a remnant of the greatness of our original nature, which teaches them that happiness in reality consists only in rest, and not in stir. And of these two contrary instincts they form within themselves a confused idea, which hides itself from their view in the depths of their soul, inciting them to aim at rest through excitement. . . .[39]

The same self-deceit prevails in the psychology of "having" as in the psychology of "doing":

> This man spends his life without weariness in playing every day for a small stake. Give him each morning the money he can win each day, on condition he does not play; you make him miserable. It will perhaps be said that he seeks the amusement and not the winnings. Make him then play for nothing; he will not become excited, and will feel bored.[40]

The self-deceit is in the fact that "He must be excited over it, and deceive himself by the fancy that he will be happy to win what he would not have as a gift on condition of not playing. . . ." [41]

> Thus so wretched is man that he would weary even without any cause for weariness from the peculiar state of his disposition; and so frivolous is he, that . . . the least thing, such as playing billiards or hitting a ball, is sufficient to amuse him.[42]

Pascal's "diversion" is close to Sartre's "self-deceit" inasmuch as it involves the duplicity of the self, yet it is closer basically to Heidegger's "inauthentic existence." Heidegger's inauthenticity consists in refusing to face one's existence in its entirety, culminating in death as our most personal possibility ("We shall die alone," says Pascal) while Sartrean self-deceit rather consists in refusing to face a liberty grounded somehow in nothingness. The result is the same insofar as our relations with others are concerned; the inauthenticity of our lives is related to our need to live an imaginary existence in the minds of others, and this need is itself related to an inauthentic conception of time, particularly in Heidegger, whose views on social life seem very close to Pascal. As in Heidegger, so in Pascal, we escape the present in the near future:

> The present is never our end. The past and the present are our means; the future alone is our end. So we never live, but we hope to live; and, as we are always preparing to be happy, it is inevitable we should never be so.[43]

Pascal's conclusion is that:

> The only thing which consoles us for our miseries is diversion, and yet this is the greatest of our miseries. For it is this which principally hinders us from reflecting upon ourselves, and which makes us insensibly ruin ourselves. Without this we should be in a state of weariness, and this weariness would spur us to seek a more solid means of escaping from it.[44]

Both Heidegger and Sartre have enormously enriched and systematized the treatment of all the themes encountered so far, as they transferred them from the plane of "convergent digressions" to the plane of discursive thought. These themes, dealing generally with the limitations of the human condition, are summed up by Pascal under the heading of "Misery of man without God." To Pascal however, through a sort of dialectical process which will be further defined later, the thought of man's misery irresistibly evokes that of man's greatness; and to begin with the very situation of man lost in the immensity of the universe: "By space the universe encompasses me and swallows me up like an atom; by thought I comprehend the world."[45] This statement, in its brevity, throws a sharp light on the meaning of Heidegger's *Dasein*: man is in the world but in some way the world is in man. As consciousness of his situation, he transcends that situation. As interpreted by Sartre in his humanistic mood, this simply means that man is not in the world as a stone or a vegetable are there. As to animals, Pascal is struck by the repetitious character of their behavior and, like Bergson, sees in instinct and reason "the marks of two natures." [46]

Truly man is "for death," like the rest of the animal kingdom, but man knows it:

> Man is but a reed, the most feeble in nature; but he is a thinking reed. The entire universe need not arm itself to crush him. . . . But, if the universe were to crush him, man would still be more noble than that which killed him, because he knows that he dies and the advantage which the universe has over him; the universe knows nothing of this.[47]

Malraux will go further and state that of all animals man is the only one that knows that he is going to die.

The very fact that man is dissatisfied with the limitations of his existence is sufficient proof that there is an element of infinity immanent in his nature: "The greatness of man is great in that he knows itself to be miserable. A tree does not know itself to be miserable." [48] Man's misery is that of a dispossessed king. Furthermore, man shows, by the importance he gives to the esteem of others, that he recognizes in them the same element of infinity: "We have so great an idea of the soul of man that we cannot endure being despised, or not being esteemed by any soul. . . ." [49] No matter how man may try to depreciate the opinion of others, he is not satisfied unless he has their esteem: "And those who most despise men, and put them on a level with the brutes, yet wish to be admired and believed by men, and contradict themselves by their own feelings. . . ." [50] The twofold nature of man is evident from his wretchedness: "For what in animals is nature we call in men wretchedness; by which we recognize that, his nature being now like that of animals he has fallen from a better nature which once was his." [51] Yet this two-fold nature is one that he has to assume: "Man is neither angel nor brute, and the unfortunate thing is that he who would act the angel acts the brute." [52] Fully to understand this celebrated statement, one should remember that Pascal believes in the logical necessity of a certain dialectical process related to man's situation in the chain of being:

> Nature has set us so well in the center, that if we change one side of the balance, we change the other too. . . . This makes me believe that the springs in our brain are so adjusted that he who touches one touches also its contrary. [53]

It is in such insistence on the rejection of both idealism and materialism that existentialism has affinities with humanism; in a somewhat similar way, Sartre claims that idealism leads to materialism and materialism to idealism. Thinking in terms of passions, i.e., of a form of behavior that brings man close to the automatism of animal instinct, Pascal remarks that the war of reason against passions "has made a division of those who would have peace into two sects. The first would renounce their passions, and become gods; the others would renounce reason, and become brute beasts." [54] But, of course, neither has been successful. Pascal will not allow his reader this kind of escape. By humiliating him and exalting him in turn, he aims at obliging him to recognize the two opposite poles of his nature, which is that of an "incomprehensible monster" only to be explained through the dogma of the Fall. The voice of Pascal, now become the voice of God, tells man of man's original sin:

> He wanted to make himself his own center. . . . I abandoned him to himself. And setting in revolt the creatures that were subject to him, I made them his enemies; so that man is now become like the brutes, and so estranged from me that there scarce remains to him a dim vision of his author. [55]

There is no injustice in the fact that we must suffer for a sin that we have not committed, for we are born unjust insofar as our will tends to self, and our existence is our guilt. The sense of an existential guilt, inseparable from existence, is related by Heidegger to the acceptance of finitude, and by Sartre to the co-existence of several selves, constituting several absolute centers of reference. In this case, it is Sartre who is closer to Pascal.

We have been able so far to ask Pascal to elucidate for us, in the clear and forceful style of seventeenth-century humanism, most of the main themes of modern existentialism; we had to leave aside a number of secondary themes, and this inquiry is far from exhaustive. If Heidegger and Sartre do not give the same answers to the riddle of existence as Pascal, they at least raise the same questions. Heidegger, however, evokes Pascal not only through his basic themes and details of minute observation, but also through a similar kind of obscure poetry and feeling.

This might be due to the mere logical necessity involved from the start in the existential position; but the connection might also be more direct. The only decoration of Heidegger's study consisted of the picture of Pascal, together with that of the poet Hölderlin. In the encounter of these two portraits over Heidegger's desk, we might perhaps detect the symbolic conjunction of French Jansenist humanism with German romanticism; the meeting of two divergent currents of western thought may not seem so paradoxical if we note the apparent persistence, in Pascal's Augustinianism, of its Neo-Platonic source, which is also that of romanticism and of modern vitalism. It is very largely through Heidegger that these two currents also meet in Sartre.

The parallel stops there. Pascal concludes his penetrating analysis of the human condition with the statement that after facing it the most rational step to take is the leap into the irrationality of Christian revelation; Heidegger and Sartre seek their absolute respectively in the notion of Being and in the notion of Non-Being.

3. THE IMAGE OF MAN IN ONTOLOGICAL HUMANISM

In Heidegger and Sartre indeed, the notion of Being seems to replace the notion of God. Heidegger seeks the Being of being (absolute Being in existential being) in the same way as Augustine sought the reflection of God's image in man's mind. The notion of pure Being, neither this, nor that, nor anything imaginable, is, as we know, hardly distinguishable from its opposite, the notion of Non-Being. In Plotinus, as *The One*, it is the superessential Non-Being which is the source of all determinate being. Heidegger seems to come back to this notion when he wonders whether Being and Non-Being are not identical. His quest has not enlightened us much on the ultimate mystery of Being, but it has indeed thrown much light on the "regions of being" accessible to the human reality.

Sartre's Being is more ambiguous. Limiting himself to his phenomenological approach, considering only what appears to consciousness. Sartre makes pure Being appear before consciousness as "the phenomenon of Being," only to dismiss it as "pre-reflective consciousness," and it is this pre-reflective consciousness which is directly experienced in nausea or boredom. Thus, with Sartre, the ultimate realities of an intelligible heaven are finally ignored, and replaced with the ultimate reality of immediate consciousness, which is after all an existential absolute; but this self-consciousness soon turns out to be a nothingness which could not be understood without the foundation of the being which it negates, and this being, or being-in-itself, in turn seems to correspond to what empirical experience, or common sense, designates as being. Self-consciousness, or pre-reflective being-for-itself, on the other hand, neither this, nor that, nor anything imaginable, becomes on closer analysis an absolute negation, a pure Non-Being, and it is in the light of this absolute that Sartre proceeds with his amazing analysis of the "human reality." While his Non-Being appears to be an absolute, somehow accessible to the human mind, we lack a metaphysical dimension in his "being-in-itself." This dimension is merely suggested in the few pages of *Being and Nothingness* devoted to "metaphysical perspectives," and these pages indeed leave us the notion that his being-in-itself is itself the result of a long process of disintegration, starting with motion, which is already a "lesser being," to end with the irruption of Non-Being into Being as consciousness.

Whatever the source of consciousness may be, there it is, an absolute Non-Being, and the only absolute accessible to man. We may then wonder whether this pure Non-Being, which is the source of our liberty is very different from Heidegger's Being, or for that matter, from the superessential Being of Plotinus, or from Brahma, defined by William James as a Non-Being charged with all the possibilities.

Whatever its provenience, this Non-Being, secreted by Being, is not to be sought in Heaven but in the self. It is ultimate reality, and it is the origin of man's liberty, to be experienced in solitude and in anguish, for, if we can recognize it in others, we cannot share it with them; in Sartre as in Pascal, the self, or consciousness, "makes itself the center of the world," the only difference being that in Sartre it is on the plane of action, as the absolute center of reference of a totalitarian organization of the world. As in Pascal, it is therefore "unjust" (or, in Sartre's words, "scandalous") if not by its nature (since in Sartre man has no nature) at least by its central location, and "inconvenient" to other selves, since they also make themselves the center of the world. In this scandalous situation, Sartre sees the source of existential guilt and the explanation of the original sin. To Sartre, as to Pascal: "we are born unjust." Although there is no common human nature to serve as the basis of Sartrean humanism, there is still a human condition, which all men share, to serve the same purpose and confer upon it universal validity.

As in Pascal, so in Sartre, man's misery is also his greatness, since it is man's consciousness which makes him miserable by making him free and allowing him to transcend his situation.

Yet, also as in Pascal, man is only free from the situation which he has to assume in guilt. Assuming the human condition, instead of fleeing it in inauthentic life, is part of any philosophy of existence. In Pascal, however, it is assumed in the light of a transcendental value which does not exist in Sartre. This transcendental value, which is the notion of God, is rejected by Sartre insofar as it involves the notion of creation *ex nihilo,* an illusion derived by *homo faber* from the process of fabrication, and encourages the surrender of personal consciousness to a divine subjectivity.

The only real value left to Sartrean humanism is liberty from a situation which involves the human condition as well as the contingency of a particular situation. The situation is to be assumed and given a meaning, but it is up to man to choose the meaning. Obviously, this meaning could be no other, ideally, than the liberty of all, but the notion of liberty as an absolute value involves in its turn a number of theoretical as well as practical difficulties.

Sartrean humanism restores man's dignity, threatened by the numerous modern disciplines which tend to make of him a psychic mechanism, by relating his sense of liberty to an absolute which gives it a philosophical justification, but it is an absolute of Non-Being.

It suggests the possibility of a system of ethics which would stem from the recognition of the same absolute in the consciousness of others, but this recognition is on the plane of conflict.

It does indeed offer some hope for the possibility of a compromise which might do away with the "inconvenience" of this situation, but the solution, the common management of the planet, is on the plane of action and beyond the scope of this essay.

We must ask from Sartre's humanism only what it can give: for lack of some sort of positive metaphysical absolute, it brings us a new, illuminating, and fascinating study of the operation of liberty based on negative values, and constitutes an immense catharsis of the unrecognized dangers of our objective society.

4

The Scandal of Multiplicity of Consciousnesses

Self is hateful. You Milton, conceal it; you do not for that reason
destroy it; you are, then, always hateful.
—No; for in acting as we do to oblige everybody, we give no more
occasion for hatred of us.—That is true, if we only hated in Self the vexa-
tion which comes to us from it. But if I hate it because it is unjust, and
because it makes itself the center of everything, I shall always hate it.

PASCAL

I. CULPABILITY AND PSYCHIC PLURALITY

The feeling of a fundamental guilt attached to the
very fact of existence is common to all forms of existentialism. In
Christian existentialism, this feeling can be explained by the
dogma of the Fall. In Sartrean existentialism as in certain
mystical currents of the Neo-Platonic tradition, it is associated
with the multiplicity of consciousnesses. We need not wonder
why theology and philosophy may sometimes meet on the existential plane, until they face the mystery of the *other,* which
marks the point of their divergence. As philosophy fell under
the sway of scientific disciplines, religion alone attended to
man's concern about his existence. Existentialism, finding its
first impulse in the Platonic and Augustinian branch of Christianity, merely retrieved what properly belonged to philosophy.
On what ground, however, may "atheistic" existentialism explain
the feeling of culpability outside of any biblical or Freudian interpretation?

For Heidegger, the feeling of culpability springs from the existent's realization of his original finitude. Facing an infinity of possible actions, the immense majority of which must necessarily remain unaccomplished and therefore appear to him as non-being, he is responsible for this non-being. "Being willing to exist, he makes himself responsible for his finitude. He becomes, henceforward, guilty in his very existence, fundamentally at fault."[1] Death alone can give an authentic meaning to his existence, as the last musical note, rebounding on all others, confers upon the melody its definite character. Living for death is authentic existence, but others help us to forget authentic existence in small talk, curiosity, or equivocation, and thereby to fall into the inauthentic existence of "das man," i.e., of the abstract, impersonal, interchangeable and unreal human being aimed at by social disciplines, conventions, and signs. In this philosophy of definitely Pascalian overtones, the notion of culpability is bound up with that of our responsibility for the acceptance of a given finitude among the infinity of possibles, negation of which possibles constitutes a non-being.

According to Sartre, the feeling of culpability in man does not spring from the fact that he has allowed himself, through the inauthentic existence which he assumed with the other, to forget that he has been cast into an authentic existence limited by birth and death, but from the fact that he finds himself cast into finite existence facing the other.

> It is from that singular situation that the notion of culpability and sin seems to derive its origin. It is facing the other that I am guilty. Guilty first when, under his glance, I experience my alienation and my nakedness as a fall which I must assume; this is the meaning of the famous: "They knew that they were guilty" in the Scripture. Guilty furthermore when, in my turn, I look at the other, because, by the very fact that I affirm my self, I constitute him as object and as instrument and bring to him that alienation which he will have to assume. Thus, original sin is my surge into a world where there is the other, and, whatever my ulterior re-

lations with the other may be, they will only be deviations from the original theme of my culpability.[2]

The difference which we note here between the two viewpoints comes from the fact that Heidegger's conception of the *Mitsein* does not take into account the "nihilating" character of consciousness while Sartre's being-for-others can constitute itself only by negating that it is the other's consciousness. Furthermore—and we shall see later how this concept is tied up in Sartre with that of our being-in-the-word—a consciousness could not face another consciousness without conferring upon it the character of object or abdicating for itself that of subject. Sartre admits, like most sociologists, that the individual can be conceived as individual only from the starting point of the totality of beings, but the relation which connects him with the totality is, according to Sartre, a negative relation. The dialectics which he seems to have borrowed from Hegel's *Phenomenology* is turned by him against the Hegelian philosophy of the totality.

> . . . I can indeed transcend myself toward an All, but not establish myself in that All to contemplate myself and contemplate others. No logical or epistemological optimism could bring to a close the scandal of multiplicity of consciousnesses.[3]

2. PHILOSOPHICAL DATA OF THE PROBLEM

To understand the fundamental character of the conflict involved, according to Sartre, in the original relation between one consciousness and another, we should adopt his position between Idealism and Realism. Having rejected the Hegelian viewpoint of the totality to come back to that of the Cartesian *cogito* and of Kierkegaardian subjectivity, without completely giving up the dialectical method, he brings himself to concede to Berkeley that the world exists only inasmuch as perceived by consciousness, but infers that consciousness could not exist either, without the world which it reflects. Not to confuse itself with the object reflected, consciousness indeed must deny its identity with the object reflected. Consciousness is that negation. However, starting from the negative act by which it makes itself a mere "presence" to that which it is not, consciousness organizes the world into a totality, according to its ends. It is thanks to consciousness that there is world, and that world is mostly, for each consciousness, the sum total of all the tools which it can use to realize its possibilities. In the daily encounter of human glances, each one may get an intuition of this fact as he feels himself becoming an object in a foreign world. "The fact that the Other cannot be defined otherwise than through a totalitarian organization of the world and that he is the key to that organization" as an "autonomous and intra-mondane center of reference of my world" [4] constitutes no doubt only one aspect of the problem, but this aspect offers its most striking illustration for the purpose of this essay. It implies a psychological vision corresponding to the theory of relativity, according to which there is no measurement except from a center of reference determined by the presence of an observer. We do not have to follow Sartre in his quest of a solution to the problem on the metaphysical plane. Whether or not the plurality of consciousnesses refers to an original totality of Mind, the fact remains that there is no absolute center of reference outside of individual consciousness.

3. "HELL IS THE OTHERS"

By stating that "Hell is the others," does Sartre simply mean that "others are Hell?" Are we dealing with a hypothesis concerning the afterlife or with an allegory of life? No doubt both. That the characters of the drama may survive in the consciousness of the living is quite consistent with the views of Sartre, but that they may, from the balcony of their Hell, become the powerless witnesses of that survival is much less so. Their situation can only be understood under the guise of a dramatic convention allowing us to concentrate all our attention on the problem of the other's existence. No exit is left through the usual escapes of unauthentic existence: adoption of the life of *das man,* collective masochism as objects in the consciousness of the Master, postulation of the Other as the anthropomorphic God, the togetherness engendered by a common task, our very "presence" to the world of possible commitments. An allegory of life thus cut off from its possibilities is certainly no more than an abstraction. But that abstraction allows a clear delineation of a real situation: the multiplicity of consciousnesses and their incompatibility as absolute centers of reference.

The problem, in its barest form, is presented to us on the plane of pure and simple *being* deprived of any means of flight toward the possible through temporalization. The disappearance of the instant, through which the existent makes himself present to the world, disclaiming by right of the non-being within him that he is the world, is symbolically signified by the fact that, in Hell, the waiter has no eyelids: ". . . we used to flick our eyelids. A wink we used to call it. A small black flash, a curtain going up and down; cut out from it all, the eye gets damp, the world is blacked out." [5]

The chips are down. Life is now completed, full and compact, between the absurd contingency of birth and death, like the bronze bust of Barbedienne congealed in the implacable realism of seriousness that things dictate. It would be as futile to try and get loose from that mass as for a mere spirit to try and lift up the bust. Death itself could not give to life the meaning which a final note gives to a melody; death itself comes from outside and remains contingent in spite of its definitive character. No wonder it may appear to us under the form of a Second Empire drawing-room with red and green sofas; one absurdity is as good as another. Outside of time and space, consciousnesses are going to face each other. There will have to be three of them, of course. It takes no more to build up a complete Hell. We can predict what kind of drama is going to start. Sartre gave us its complete description in *Being and Nothingness.*

In the presence of the other two damned souls, Garcin realizes that Hell might be nothing else than the multiplicity of consciousnesses. It is a question of managing the situation through a complicity of politeness among the damned. Each one will build up for himself a factitious personality in the spirit of the others. But you can build up an imaginary character for yourself in the mind of others only by justifying that fiction later on in deeds. This effort is bound to fail. The next solution to be proposed will be solipsism: let each one shut himself within the world of his memories. In order to detach herself from its full and completed existence, one of the characters, Estelle, asks for a mirror. It is not possible in Hell to pass, through the mirror of consciousness, into an imaginary gallery from which one may contemplate oneself as a mere spectator and dissociate oneself from oneself. Moreover—the mirror assumes here a dual symbolical function—there are in Hell no utensils suggesting a depersonalized consciousness of others in which one may recognize himself as "others" see him: "When I talked, I used to manage so that there might be one [mirror] around, in which I could look at myself. I talked, I saw myself talking. I saw myself as people saw me." [6] All of which the third character, Inès, fully understands when she offers to serve Estelle as a mirror, i.e., to play the part of a foreign consciousness in which Inès will feel herself living, as children do in the omniscience of the parents, believers in the look of God, to find there the free foundation which she could not find in her own consciousness, to exist as an essence, instead of just being her mere existence. The offer was merely a snare. The other had turned into a mirror just to be looked at:

Smile to me. I am not ugly either. Am I not something better than a mirror? [7] Impossible, she has become a mere look. One cannot be at once subject and object for the other. All she can do is to make use of the dependency in which she has placed Estelle: a sort of blackmailing which now turns to sadism: "My little lark, I have got you . . . Suppose the mirror now began to lie?

Or if I just closed my eyes, if I refused to look at you, what would you do with all your beauty?" [8] This last attempt fails from the fact that a third consciousness, that of Garcin, reflects at once the mirror and the object it reflects. To the eyes of that witness, the mirror is no longer reflecting; it becomes in its turn a reflected object. The painful effort of the couple to live in a closed world—we had entered the private domain of the couple, the desert of love, and stealthily returned to the plane of living— comes to naught just because another world has just superposed itself upon that world, with a new center of reference which breaks up all its perspectives. Against that witnessing consciousness, the sadistic woman now turns her resentment. It is for Inès a matter of mastering Garcin by showing him that she knows "what makes him tick," that he is for her a psychic mechanism, a thing, or more exactly, to use Sartre's language, a subject-object, a transcended-transcendence: "And the kid, she is no concern of yours, either? I saw you operate: just to get her interested, that's why you put on that grand manner of yours." [9] It is no use for Garcin to defend himself, he is wrong to exist, he is one too many—*de trop*:

> No use hiding in your corner of the sofa, you are everywhere, sounds reach me soiled by your hearing them pass by. You stole from me my very face: you know it and I don't. And what about her? You stole her from me: if we were alone, do you think she would dare to treat me as she is treating me? [10]

Meanwhile, the three damned souls still cling to the image of themselves which they have left on earth in the minds of the living, with whom they seem to have kept in touch. They realize that the image is now definitive, that they can bring no change to it. If they want to touch it up, they will have to transfer it first to the consciousness of their companions in Hell. They confess their crimes to each other: their [as many] unsuccessful attempts to solve the problems of the *other* in sadism, masochism, and flight.

Estelle, who shows signs of masochism, wants to lose herself in the consciousness of Garcin, who now dominates the situation. Garcin accepts that submission with the hope of finding in the eyes of Estelle an image of himself which will justify him. She can only refuse to reflect that image since she sees in him only a reflection of herself:

Garcin. . . . . Estelle, am I a coward?
Estelle. But I don't know, my love, I am not under your skin. It's for you to decide.[11]

Estelle finally seems to be willing to see Garcin as he wants to be seen, but it is only to reach her own ends. Inès, become a witness in her turn, now dominates the couple by all the lucidity of her consciousness, denounces its illusions and bad faith, and pursues Estelle and Garcin with her sarcasms.

Garcin wants to run away; yet, when the door opens, he stays because he cannot detach himself from the image of himself that he is leaving in the consciousness of his mates in Hell—an image which has become for him his only reality: "I could not [he confesses to Inès] leave you here, triumphant, with all those thoughts in your head: all those thoughts that concern me." [12]

He is now going to try and convince Inès that he is not a coward. She takes advantage of the situation to crush him. Estelle sees in this new development an opportunity to resume her intrigue with Garcin and suggests that he avenge himself by kissing her and making Inès jealous. The Garcin-Estelle couple is formed again, the sarcasms of Inès are resumed, and the characters understand that the same drama will unfold without end and that "Hell is Others."

No Exit is a drama aiming, by its general structure, at a concentration which leaves far behind that of a Racine play, or of Ibsen's *Doll's House*. Its close, suffocating atmosphere suggests the gas chamber. It is the perfect antithesis of the theater of escape, so popular during the Interwar period, in so far as it leaves no escape, and stands in absolute opposition to the tendencies of the *avant garde* toward a surrealism reached through the conjunction of dream and reality. Or, rather, if one prefers, since any form of neoclassicism has to rest on some anterior romanticism, *No Exit* is a synthesis of both on a single plane which excludes counterpoint effects. It may seem ill-becoming to apply the historical method to an existentialist play; but a temporary return to the drama of crisis was almost unavoidable, even without world conflict and occupation, after twenty years of poetical realism, of lyrical fancy, and of Giraudoux. The formula for a new integration remained an individual affair: if Sartre retained from the Inter-war *avant-garde* the privilege of situating his dramas in the World Beyond, a certain familiarity with the gods, and a contempt for metaphysical—or biological—discretion, it is merely for the sake of an intellectual structure in which lyricism loses its power of expansion. The movement of the play is circular, like Sartrean dialectics; it is a play of reflections mirrored within a closed field. Aside from the visions which connect the characters with the earth, the play is "closed" in form, as it is in content.

Strangely enough, the form assumed by Sartre's treatment of the same theme in *The Reprieve* is calculated to produce in the reader an impression of absolute dispersion. It is, of course, the simultaneist technique, borrowed from Dos Passos but used for a different end. Roughly speaking, we are dealing in Dos Passos with a Hegelian view of the totality distorted by Marx, and in Sartre with Hegelian dialectics as revised by Kierkegaard: on one side the movement of the masses, determined by implacable material forces, a movement registered by the "camera eye" and presented to the rhythm of the newsreel; on the other, a "detotalized totality" of consciousness which, in the simultaneous bursting apart of "instants," brings to existence as many incompatible worlds. On both sides, a certain dose of artificiality. The "camera eye" of Dos Passos has to assume the character of a transcendental consciousness to register from outside a view of the totality, and in so doing it turns all consciousnesses into psychic objects. Sartre adopts individual consciousnesses as absolute centers of reference, sees the world through their eyes, refuses to objectify them as if he were some omniscient God, and thereby manages to render the separateness of consciousnesses which the eye of the victor has not yet reduced to common objectification within an alienated world; but his method still involves a degree of artificiality inasmuch as the central character's world is seen from inside, while the world of the drafted shepherd, or the world of the prostrate invalid, is a mere conjecture on the part of the author. Here again, it is as an expository method for the literary presentation of a philosophical idea that we must consider Sartre's astonishing technique.

In his description of the bursting apart of consciousnesses "on reprieve," in this parcelled-out universe, at times the surge of the Other's existence appears under the form of anguished apprehension and insecurity within the crowd:

> The war was over there, at the end of the rails, it did not bother him, he felt threatened by a much more immediate catastrophe: crowds are perishable, there is always some disaster soaring above them. . . .[13]

Depersonalized and hypostatized as an absolute, the everpresent consciousness of the Other turns into the objectifying look of an anthropomorphic God, as in this description of a praying butcher:

> One sees him, one sees his harshness as I see his hands, his avarice as I see his scanty hair and that scanty pity shining under avarice as his skull shines through his hair; he knows it. . . . he will groan: Lord, Lord, I am a miser. And the Medusa's look will fall from above, petrifying. Virtues of stone, vices of stone: how restful.[14]

Now and then, consciousnesses confront each other in private conflicts, sink into solipsism or "inauthentic life"; yet it is less the idea of conflict than the intuition of a multiplicity of incompatible worlds that the author tries to communicate through *The Reprieve,* and he accomplishes this *tour de force:* the scandal of multiplicity of consciousnesses is never mentioned; yet it is somehow suggested through the expressive force of a technique adapted to that end.

It is enlightening to compare the method adopted by Simone de Beauvoir in her novels to illustrate the same concept. On this point, as on many others, the disciple is more explicit than the master, and takes care to elucidate, on the plane of existentialist philosophy, the psychology of her characters. This is how one of them defines her consciousness as an absolute center of reference:

> I always felt that, even as a kid: my looking at it was enough for that boulevard to exist. My voice is enough for the world to have a voice. When the world keeps quiet, it's my fault . . . I haven't created the world, but I recreate it every moment by my presence.[15]

It is in Simone de Beauvoir that the scandal of multiplicity of consciousnesses is the more clearly delineated:

> . . . it had happened, she at last had met with that unsurmountable obstacle, the premonition of which she had experienced in vague ways from her earliest childhood: through Xavière's lust for pleasure, through her hatred and jealousy, the scandal was glaring, as monstrous, as definitive as death; facing Françoise, yet without her, something existed like a condemnation without appeal: a free, absolute, irreducible foreign consciousness was standing up to her. Like death, a total negation, an eternal absence, and still, through a staggering contradiction, that abyss of nothingness could render itself present to itself and make itself exist for itself with plenitude; the whole universe was engulfed in it, and Françoise, for ever dispossessed of the world, felt herself dissolving in that void, the infinite contour of which no word, no image could delineate.[16]

The sensation described here is analyzed further on by another character:

. . . Do you still sense Xavière's existence as a scandal? . . . it is true that each one experiences his own consciousness as an absolute. How could several absolutes be compatible? It is as mysterious as birth and death. It is even such a problem that no philosophy can bite into it.[17]

That problem is the very subject of *She Came to Stay*. Because she ignored it, the heroine of the novel created around herself a private Hell: "Ah yes, said Xavière, and she shuddered. We were at the bottom of Hell, I thought we would never come out of it."[18]

On the ethical plane, however, Simone de Beauvoir suggests a solution that Sartre had not allowed us to foresee: ". . . between us there is reciprocity, said Pierre . . . From the moment that you recognize me as a consciousness, you know that I recognize you as such. That changes everything."[19] That statement we must now examine, by way of conclusion, and compare it with the practical teachings which seem to come out of Sartre's works.

4. THE ETHICAL PROBLEM

Simone de Beauvoir indeed seems to have assumed the responsibility of publishing the treatise of existentialist ethics promised by Sartre at the close of *Being and Nothingness*. Before the publication of *For an Ethics of Ambiguity,* however, *The Flies* and *The Blood of Others* had already delineated some forms of authentic behavior toward oneself, the others, and God, who, in Sartre's system, seems to represent the Other in depersonalized form. It is difficult to separate these three problems.

In *The Flies,* the problems of personal commitment, of social ethics, of the regard due to the life of others, and of obedience to God seem to blend and resolve into that of the consciousness of others. The tyrant Egistheus takes advantage of the feeling of guilt innate in the hearts of his subjects, as in the heart of every man, to reduce them to the masochism of voluntary servitude. It is the very crime by which he assumed power that he seems to want the inhabitants of Argos to expiate; in reality, they prefer the cruelty of the tyrant to the anguish which would bring them face to face with the human condition and its responsibilities. Jupiter, the incarnation of the Other's consciousness, maintains them within that servitude. Electra, who has so consciously dedicated her life to a project of vengeance that she cannot carry it out, represents a Hamlet-like attitude which does not concern us here. Orestes, a free and empty consciousness, kept available to all possibilities by a Gidean tutor, assumes responsibility for the crime which will liberate the city and murders Egistheus, together with his own mother, Clytemnestra. He does it without the help of Jupiter, who is willing to help him, providing he maintains the population in that state of fear which is favorable to the existence of the gods. Orestes leaves the city, having made to the inhabitants the gift of liberty, and the furies of remorse cling to his footsteps:

> Your faults and your remorses, your anguish at night, the crime of Egistheus, all that is now mine, I take it all on myself. Do not fear your dead, they are my dead. And see: your faithful flies have left you to follow me. But have no fear, people of Argos: I shall not sit, all covered with blood, on the throne of my victim: a god offered me that and I said no. I wish to be a king without a land and without kingdom.[20]

To elucidate the allegory of this ending, we merely have to quote the conclusion of *The Blood of Others;* the resistance hero is meditating upon the body of the innocent whom he has sent to death in a dangerous mission:

> He looked at the bed. For you, just an innocent stone: you had made your choice. Those who will be shot to-morrow will not have so chosen; I am the rock that crushes them; I shall not escape the curse: for ever I shall remain for them another, for ever I shall be for them the blind force of fate, for ever apart from them. Yet may I just devote myself to defend that supreme good which renders innocent and futile all the stones and all the rocks, that good which saves every man from all others and from myself:

liberty; then my passion will not have been useless. You did not give me peace; but why should I want peace? You gave me the courage to accept for ever risk and anguish, to bear the weight of my crimes and of the remorse which will tear me apart without end. There is no other road.[21]

The fundamental ideas illustrated by the two passages are developed in *For an Ethics of Ambiguity:* Each consciousness is an absolute, each consciousness recreates the world every moment, "the other, at each instant, is stealing from me the entire world," [22] and it is indeed true that, as Hegel claims, "each consciousness pursues the death of the other." [23] But, on the other side, each consciousness is bound up with the others through the very act by which it distinguishes itself from them: "each man needs the liberty of other men and, in a sense, he always wants it, were he a tyrant; he merely fails to assume in good faith the consequences of such a will." [24] An existential system of ethics would be that which would assign as the aim of all actions the liberty of man, that liberty through which he would assume his existence "in its finitude open on infinity." [25]

At this point arises the eternal question of ends and means, and the ethics of ambiguity becomes somewhat ambiguous ethics. On one hand, each consciousness must be treated as an end, as in Kantian ethics; but on the other, in the course of the conflict for the liberation of consciousnesses, individuals and even whole generations may have to be treated as means to an end. One does not govern in innocence. It is up to the leader to decide, but whatever he does he must remember that the end does not justify the means, be resigned to bear alone the weight of his crimes, answer for the blood of others, be willing to see the furies cling to his steps. Power does not constitute a delegation of responsibility to divine or historical forces:

Since the liberation aimed at is not a thing situated in an alien time, but a movement which is realized as it tends toward self-mastery, it cannot be attained if it first disavows itself: action

cannot seek its fulfillment through means which would destroy its
very meaning.[26]

Moreover, if others are also free, we could not be absolutely certain of the consequences of our acts. This is what Sartre tried to
prove in *Dirty Hands,* and Huxley in *Grey Eminence.* For Sartre
as for Huxley, ends and means constitute a single movement and
the means condition the end.

A doctrine which makes of the relations between consciousnesses an irreducible conflict may seem exaggeratedly pessimistic.
Let us note, however, that by making of individual consciousness
an absolute, and by setting liberty at the core of that absolute,
it leads to the respect of the human person and constitutes indeed,
as Sartre claims, a form of humanism. Moreover, the social philosophy which may best help to solve the problem of actual conflicts between liberties is not that which theoretically denies the
existence of the problem, only to recognize it implicitly in all
forms of action, as is very commonly the case. A new optimism
ought to come out purified from the test imposed by Sartrean
dialectics; but, no doubt, it will have to abandon the quest of
being-for-others on the plane of pure being for quest of being-
with-others on the plane of action, a possibility which the author
of *Being and Nothingness* acknowledges to a certain degree in
this description of the "we" defined as the team spirit:

> . . . the rhythm which I bring to life is born in conjunction with
> me and laterally as collective rhythm; it is my rhythm to the
> degree that it is their rhythm and conversely. This is precisely
> the ground of the experience of the "we"; it is finally our rhythm.
> . . . And no doubt, that experience of the "we" may be sought as
> the symbol of an absolute and metaphysical unity of all tran-
> scendences; it seems, indeed, that it suppresses the original con-
> flict of transcendences by making them converge toward the world;
> in that sense, the ideal "we" would be the "we" of a humanity
> which would achieve domination of the earth. But the experience
> of the "we" remains on the ground of individual psychology as a
> mere symbol of the desirable unity of transcendences; it is in no

way, indeed, a lateral and real apprehension of subjectivities as such by a single subjectivity; the subjectivities remain out of reach and radically separated. . . . I learn that I am part of a "we" through the world.[27]

A big admission it is, nevertheless, to grant the possible mediation, between free conscious beings, of a world unified through common action.[28]

5

Existential Symbolism

The symbol represents the dream of a non-destructive assimilation.

L'Etre et le Néant

I. SARTRE'S THEORY OF EXISTENTIAL SYMBOLISM

Sartre has devoted no special treatise to existential symbolism, but this term is used and made explicit in several chapters of *L'Etre et le Néant*.

Existential symbolism expresses primarily the craving of consciousness for being. Sartrean consciousness, one may recall, is intentional, negative, free, and transcendent. It is intentional in that it aims at things, which are not in consciousness, even in a degraded form. It is negative in that it distinguishes itself from the thing aimed at, and is in fact nothing more than that negation, i.e., a pure non-being; free because, as non-being, it escapes the law of causality; transcendent, since, being a mere presence to that which it is not, it projects itself as future presence to that which it is not yet. Sartre leaves us with the conception of a free consciousness, forever disconnected with being, yet in desperate quest of a foundation which it might give itself freely. Freud's *libido* and Adler's will-to-power are specific and secondary aspects of the craving of consciousness for being.[1]

This craving may manifest itself directly, as in the reflective process, through which consciousness tries to objectify its own reactions, or through the existential categories of doing or having.[2] These are reducible to being. We do, or make, in order to have. Having, or appropriation, in which the thing possessed represents being for consciousness, can only be symbolical.[3] Recognition of this fact may bring about the urge to destroy. Destroying is a form of appropriation, as is consuming. Smoking tobacco, according to Sartre, is a symbolic "appropriation of the whole world."[4] Most of the time, the craving of consciousness for being operates through the world on the plane of appropriation.

Our love of a particular object, or being, fundamentally expresses our secret love of being in general:

> Each object possessed, standing out on the background of the world, makes the whole world manifest, as the loved woman makes manifest the sky, the beach, the sea which surrounded her when she appeared. To appropriate an object for oneself is therefore to appropriate the world symbolically.[5]

Why we prefer to possess the world through a certain particular object is explained thus:

> We aim in it at its *being* through its manner of being, or quality. . . . Existential psychoanalysis should make its task the making out of the *ontological* sense of qualities. It is thus only—and not through considerations of sexuality—that we shall explain, for instance, certain constant features of poetical "imaginations" (the "geological" in Rimbaud, the lucidity of water in Poe). . . .[6]

Existential symbolism is not self-projection, but a sort of revelation, claiming a form of objectivity. We wish Sartre had gone deeper into this matter but he could not have done so without metaphysical hypotheses, which would have been beyond the scope of his phenomenology, and he is satisfied with the descriptive allusions of an "as if" philosophy:

> Everything takes place as if we surged up in a universe wherein sentiments and acts are all charged with materiality, have sub-

stantial structure [*une étoffe substantielle*], are *truly* soft, flat, viscous, low, lofty, etc., and where material substances originally have a psychic significance which renders them repugnant, horrifying, attractive, etc. . . .[7]

In order to understand this "immense universal symbolism," which manifests itself through our hatred or sympathies toward objects, we should first concede that it is not based on prior experience. The child understands this symbolism in his pre-psychical and pre-sexual life:

. . . the sticky, the pasty, the vaporous, etc., holes in the sand and in the earth, caverns, light, night, etc., reveal to him pre-sexual modes of being, which he will spend his life later in rendering explicit.[8]

If, however, consciousness is free to cause certain objects, or certain qualities, to stand out on the background of perception, as demonstrated by the Gestaltists, this freedom is related to a project concerning being, or, if one prefers, to an attitude about life which may be thereby confirmed or revealed. Sartre's characters go searching among the objects of this world for the qualities, texture, color, etc., which will symbolize for them the fundamental projects they have adopted for life, secondary aspects of such projects, or the suggestion of entirely new projects. As in Baudelaire, so in Sartre, man walks along in the forest of symbols, and these symbols have objective meanings which are the same for all of us. To all of us, light suggests the transparency of consciousness; the rock, permanence and stability; water, liberty through change and flow; viscosity, our freedom being swamped by contingency; to all of us, it would seem, blue suggests the inaccessible ideal; red, action; yellow, retreat, etc. The person who says: "I feel blue because he called me yellow, and I saw red," is relying implicitly on a certain universality of meaning in the symbolism of colors, which transcends the conventionality of semantic signs.

If, however, the meanings of existential symbols are universal, the values attached to these meanings may differ according to our life-projects. We react variously to them and while they represent values to some people they may represent anti-values to others. This is no doubt the real reason why there is no possible discussion of tastes and colors.

We might, then, tentatively define Sartre's existential symbolism as objective and revealing, universal in meaning, but differing in value according to our individual life-projects.[9]

To illustrate his theory, Sartre gives in *L'Etre et le Néant* a few examples, related to what he considers the most fundamental values or anti-values of human existence:

Pure being is suggested by snow, which

> represents pure exteriority, radical spatiality. Its indifferentiation, its monotony and its whiteness manifest the absolute nudity of substance. . . . This pure in-itself, similar to the absolute and intelligible plenum of Cartesian extension, fascinates me as the pure apparition of the non-self; what I want, then, is precisely that this in-itself be related to me by a rapport of emanation while remaining itself. Such is the meaning even of the snow-men and snow-balls made by children. . . .[10]

If, in the almost abstract form of space unrelieved and untouched by life, yet opaque in its absolute purity, snow offers the best symbol of pure being, the skier's glide over snow corresponds to the effort of consciousness to appropriate that quality symbolically. Through speed, consciousness unifies that undifferentiated exteriority. It would be even better if skiing left no trace. Ideal appropriation is suggested by the quality of smoothness: "What is smooth can be taken, felt and remains none the less impenetrable. . . . This is why there is so much insistence in erotic description on the white smoothness of the feminine body." [11]

Consciousness is often symbolized by water:

> . . . its movement, its fluidity . . . its perpetual flight, everything about it recalls the for-itself to the extent that the first psychologists

who stressed the character of *duration* in consciousness (James, Bergson), very frequently compared it to a river. It is the river which best evokes the image of the constant interpenetration of the parts of a whole and of their perpetual dissociation. . . .[12]

This is why "the symbol of the body of water seems to play such an important part in the constitution of pantheistic schemes."[13]

If the ideal value of man is the triumph of being-for-itself over being-in-itself (which we may loosely conceive as the triumph of spirit over matter) his ideal anti-value is the triumph of being-in-itself over consciousness, symbolized by the quality of viscosity. This quality

represents in itself an incipient triumph of the solid over the liquid, i.e., a tendency of the indifferent in-itself which the pure liquid represents, to congeal liquidity, i.e., to absorb the for-itself which ought to ground it. . . .[14]

The viscous is "the revenge of the in-itself":

The viscous is *docile;* only, at the very moment when I think I possess it, through a curious reversal, it possesses me. . . . In a sense, it is something like the supreme docility, the faithfulness of a dog which *offers* himself when you do not want him any more; and, in another sense, it is, under that docility, a sly appropriation of the possessor by the possessed. One sees here the symbol which suddenly reveals itself. . . . there is a possibility that the in-itself may absorb the for-itself. . . .[15]

But the viscous also symbolizes the quenching of our hopes for the future by a malignant past which overtakes us:

As soon as we surge into the world, we have this obsession of a consciousness which would spring toward the future, toward a new project concerning itself; yet, at the very moment when it would be conscious of succeeding, it would feel itself being slyly and invisibly held back by the suction of the past, and would witness its slow dilution within that past which it flees. . . .[16]

In other words, our free projects, ourselves, may become "swamped" in the very course of their realization.

It is the fear, not of death, not of the pure in-itself, not of non-being, but of a particular type of being which does no more exist than the In-Itself-for-Itself. . . . an ideal being wherein the ungrounded In-Itself has priority over the For-Itself, and which we shall call an anti-value.[17]

Between the ideal value represented by the triumphant glide of the skier over the snow and the anti-value represented by the slow and sly suction exercised by some viscous matter, we find, in *L'Etre et le Néant,* few illustrations of existential symbolism. In Sartre's literary works, however, we encounter a much greater variety of symbols and can detect both their meanings and their values by the reactions of the characters to them. We must remember that the more or less acute perceptions of symbolic objects, or of the symbolic qualities of objects, are related to the life-projects adopted by the characters. We must also remember that although meanings of symbols are assumed to be universal since they refer to the universal human condition, their values will differ according to the life-project of each character. Only rarely will a character be able to psychoanalyze his own reactions and discover what his life-project really is. The role of analyst will ordinarily be assumed by some character other than the subject, or by the reader himself, who has been provided, through the complicity of the author, with clues for the analysis.

2. EXISTENTIAL SYMBOLISM ON THE PLANE OF PERCEPTION

I shall here stress symbol-perception, rather than symbol-imagining, for it constitutes a more original, direct, and striking illustration of the manner in which existential symbolism is related to behavior in Sartre's literary works.

First of all, the perception of symbolic objects varies in acuteness according to whether or not the character is ready for a new resolve.

As he realizes that his life has no future, Mathieu ceases to perceive things as meaningful: "Things have remained there intact. . . . All their customary little solicitations, all their tiny grasshoppers' songs have vanished into the air, they keep quiet." [18] Later on, he looks for a possible commitment and fails to detect the suggestion offered him by the symptoms of impending war: "Not a sign in the sky nor on the earth, the objects of this world were too absorbed in their war, they turned their manifold heads toward the east." [19] Here the absence of any sign in the sky or on the earth reflects the absence of resolve in the character. Elsewhere, the sign refuses to appear because the character is self-conscious, or insincere in his resolve, which he wants confirmed *from outside*. Daniel has decided to emasculate himself: "He asks for help, for a sign. All is inert and silent. . . ." [20]

Sometimes, a character interprets a sign in bad faith. Philippe thinks that he has a mission: to oppose the war. His rebellion against patriotism is merely adolescent negative behavior. About to leave for Switzerland, he gets drunk and finds himself in the room of a prostitute. He interprets this circumstance as a sign that he should not leave:

> The world is full of signs. Everything is a sign. One must know how to decipher them. You were to leave, you get drunk, you no longer leave; why didn't you leave? Because you didn't have to go. It's a sign. . . .[21]

Lucien, the budding fascist, is a serious man. He seeks reasons to act in the nature of things. As a disciple of Barrès, he will draw from his sacred soil the strength to become a leader: ". . . he had to study the soil and the under-soil of Ferolles, to decipher the sense of the rolling hills which slope to La Sernette." [22]

These characters are either undecided or insincere. They try to find reasons to act, or justification, in "signs" because they are incapable of facing their liberty. In authentic existential symbolism, the appearance of the symbol, the realization of a given situation, and the breaking-away from that situation under the compelling force of a new resolve, are simultaneous.

Mathieu, through one of these rare "ecstasies" which permit us to survey our whole past existence, realizes the barrenness of liberty without commitment. Standing on the Pont-Neuf, he slowly moves his hand over the stone balustrade:

> . . . There it was, enormous and massive, enclosing in itself the crushed silence, the compressed darkness which are the inside of things. There it was, a plenitude. He would have liked to cling to that stone, to fuse with it, to fill himself with its opacity, with its repose. But it could be of no help to him: it was outside, forever.[23]

The stone represents being-in-itself, with all its concrete reality, compactness, and self-identity, in contrast to Mathieu's consciousness, which is free and empty: "As inseparable from the world as light and yet exiled, like light, gliding over the surface of stones and water, without anything ever holding me or stranding me." [24] Stone and light have universal significance, but the values Mathieu attributes to them in this passage are his own; they correspond to a change of heart which will eventually alter the course of his existence. Mathieu is temporarily attracted by the concreteness and infinite repose of the stone because, fundamentally, he would like to invest his boundless liberty with these attributes.

The symbolic meaning of water is seldom exploited in Sartre's work. We find it had played a part in shaping Mathieu's ideal first ideal:

> The water was flowing through two cast iron pipes into the stone trough; it was cold and bare like a skin; all night Mathieu had heard its hopeful whispering, its childish questioning. He plunged his head into the trough, the tiny elemental song became that mute and lustrous coolness in his ears, in his nostrils, that bouquet of wet roses, of water-lilies in his heart; bathing in the Loire, the reeds, the small green island, childhood.[25]

In Mathieu's consciousness, the longing for being manifests it-self through an effort to appropriate the qualities of water: cool-ness, transparency and fluidity, which, as we know, symbolize consciousness. But Mathieu is merely reverting to a youthful dream. Water and light, then, symbolize two different kinds of liberty for Sartre. Water, the more ambiguous symbol, represents a sense of liberty expressing itself through change, restlessness, eternal questioning, eternal refusal, a desire to remain available, a sort of Gidean *disponibilité*. Light represents absolute lucidity, and with it the sense of non-being, the longing for being, an-guish, and the realization of the necessity for commitment.

The reactions of Boris to the sound of water, after a night of indulgence, are somewhat similar to Mathieu's: "The noise of water was agreeable and innocent. Boris listened to it with pleasure. Men hallucinated by thirst in the desert heard similar noises, the noises of springs." [26] To Boris, water symbolizes purity, the refusal to become involved in the life of the flesh. A mo-ment later, he will discover that he wants to be a monk; yet, the circumstances surrounding this discovery discredit his re-solve. Because his sense of purity is rather a fear of involvement, it is appropriately represented by the symbol of water.

The second definition of liberty—as anguish, longing for being, the sense of non-being—is closer to Mathieu's final con-ception of it, at least to his realization of the insubstantial char-acter of liberty for its own sake, the liberty which is, of course, pure consciousness: "The light lay in the streets and on the roofs, even, fixed, and cold as eternal truth. Is it true that I am not a skunk?" [27]

As light loses its transparency, it expresses corresponding variations in the consciousness of Sartre's characters. Whiteness imparts to light the peculiar opacity which we shall find later associated with that color: "A white light invaded the hall, it was the awakening; people were glad to find themselves together again. . . . Mathieu did not awaken, it was just a white nightmare. . . ." [28] The white light seems to symbolize here the dimness of collective thinking; at any rate, it does not suggest lucidity but the opposite.

As Gomez the painter steps out into a New York street under a blazing sun, he resents "the light, white as a catastrophe. . . ." [29] To a painter, the disappearance from the landscape of all colors, as the afternoon sun devours them, leaving in their place a whitish and luminous haze, is indeed a catastrophe, the destruction of a painter's world. Thomas Wolfe, however, mentions the same phenomenon among those best suited to suggest to "God's lonely man" the feeling of his solitude. The opacity of too bright a light often calls for the opacity of black in the imagination of Sartre's characters. To Daniel, "the sun was an artifice: a flash of magnesium which concealed night. . . ." [30] That night and day seem equivalent to Daniel, obsessed by guilt and ready for conversion, may seem natural. To George, the recruit, bright sunshine evokes death: ". . . the sun was everywhere, in the houses, in the barracks, and on the countryside. . . . He thought of the war and realized that he was not afraid to die." [31] A glaring light brings to most of Sartre's characters thoughts of darkness, disaster, or death, as in Platonist schemes terrestrial light evokes darkness by comparison with spiritual light. For Sartre, however, the absolute transparency of consciousness takes the place of the transcendental sun.

If the rock symbolizes the concreteness of the in-itself, and if light, in all its variations, contains a reference to consciousness, the viscous, as we have seen, represents the triumph of the in-itself over the for-itself, of the contingent over the transcendent, of the past over the future. Such is the meaning that viscosity will have for all of Sartre's characters, but some of them will not consider it as an anti-value:

Rirette felt a great emptiness in her head, because she was so tired, she was looking at the port wine, all viscous in her glass, like liquid caramel, and a voice repeated within her: "Happiness, happiness". . . .[32]

The emptiness in her head is of course the painful realization of her liberty; the viscous liquid evokes for her a life happily swamped by petty preoccupations.

Maurice is afraid of the war. On the boat from Algeria to Marseilles he is taken ill: "A viscous, sticky, sugary syrup, he was no longer afraid, he was no longer ashamed, it was so delightful to be sea-sick." [33]

To Mathieu, on the other hand, the viscous is definitely an anti-value:

> Mathieu breathed in a green and living fragrance, a young dust; he winked "Summer!" He took a few steps; the black melting pitch, specked with white grains, stuck to his soles: Marcelle was pregnant; it was no longer the same summer.[34]

Mathieu's assimilation of a perfectly normal process of nature to the action of melting pitch on his soles may be taken to illustrate spite at seeing one's destiny take an unexpected turn, the failure to find liberty outside of commitment, the impossibility of divorcing consciousness from existence, the triumph of life's contingency over the transcendence of consciousness, the encroachment of the past upon the future, and the ethical consideration that our acts follow us, since at any moment we are free only from a given situation. All these interpretations are aspects of the same philosophy.

As Daniel is about to drown his cats, to detach himself from his last real earthly love, he has an overpowering sensation of freedom:

> "I am free," he thought to himself. But it was an impersonal pride, for Daniel was no longer anybody. At eleven twenty-five he got up, he felt so weak that he had to lean against the barrel. He stained his tweed jacket with pitch and looked at the stain.
>
> As he saw the black stain on the purplish cloth, he suddenly felt that he was only one person. A man alone. A coward.[35]

Again liberty is depicted as an intolerable vacuum, and the suction of the past represented by the viscosity—and the blackness—of pitch. Daniel will not drown his cats, i.e., his past. It is his past which catches up with him, drowning his future projects.

Like the viscous, the pasty seems to symbolize for Sartre the opacity of being-in-itself. The pasty, like the viscous, yields to pressure as it is handled, but it is more likely to retain the form which one gives to it. Roquentin likes to roll old bits of paper between his fingers:

> . . . this morning. . . . I wanted but could not pick up a paper lying on the ground. . . . I bent down, already rejoicing at touching that fresh and tender paste which would turn under my fingers into grey pellets. . . . I could not.[36]

Longing for being, represented by this gesture of appropriative destruction and transformation, is about to change into nausea. The meaning of the fresh tender paste is still the same, but the value of this meaning has changed.

Colors seem to play the most important part in Sartrean symbolism. The use of each color fits into a rather consistent scheme.

Blue retains its Baudelairean sense: the obsession of an ideal and of its inaccessibility, but, in Sartre, the ideal has ceased to be a transcendental, spiritual reality, the ultimate reality; it is only a value. Blue symbolizes the dynamic, transcending movement of consciousness toward that value, not a Divine Idea shining through the sky's azure.

As Daniel looks for a sign to encourage him in his purpose of self-emasculation, he finds himself facing his subjectivity: "Everything is inert and silent. . . . He alone is erect, he alone alive in too blue a light." [37] Later on, in *Le Sursis,* he tries to put his consciousness to sleep, wishes he were "made of stone," would like to "extinguish the internal look," and after several ineffectual spiritual exercises, "throws a challenge at the clear sky": "Under the azure, a bitter claim, a vain supplication. . . ."

Then, at last, he feels that he is seen:

> He was *the object* of a look. A look which searched him to his inner depth, which stabbed him through and through and which was not his look; an opaque look, night in person, waiting for him there, deep inside, which condemned him to be himself, a coward, a hypocrite, a homosexual for eternity.[38]

The passage from blue to black indicates the passage from the sense of his subjectivity to the sense of his objectivity for others. Daniel has succeeded in objectifying himself in the glance of a being who is both subject and object, whom he believes to be God, but who is only the personification of *other* people, of those whose judgment reduces him to be only what he has been and still is, deprives him of his transcendence, suppresses in him the sense of liberty and anguish.

Purple is an undecided hue which, to all characters, means compromise between dreaming and acting, between the ideal and the practical: false resolutions, defeated ideals. Lulu's lover, the serious man, likes "the mauve tinge of the Paris sky."[39] Lulu uses "a thin purple sheet" to announce to a friend that she is going to resume with him a life of compromise.[40] Daniel puts on a purplish tweed as he goes to drown his cats; he really is not decided to do so. To Mathieu, purplish hues connote the failure of liberty without commitment: "A huge mauve flower was ascending towards the sky, it was night, Mathieu was walking in that night, thinking: I am a wash-out."[41]

Red is action, but in the form of unrestrained vital urges, war and crime. As Daniel is wandering through the streets of occupied Paris, the only gay note he sees in the gray city is the Nazi flag: a knot of black serpents projected," as in the circle of a lantern, on "the standard of bleeding flesh."[42] In Ivich, who has retired to Laon, the red halo surrounding the railway station precipitates an urge to live at furious pace what might be the last days of Paris: "The station was there, just below her, this red halo downstairs; the night train left at three-twenty. "I have a hundred francs," she thought triumphantly, 'I have a hundred francs in my bag.' " [43]

Orange, russet, and brown, are, like purple, ambiguous colors since they represent the transition from red to yellow which latter, as we shall see, stands for recoil and immanence. Mathieu remembers how he was deceived by the peaceful golden glow of a pre-war Italian evening while he was eating apricot ice-cream, watching the sunset:

> If I had been able to suspect, in the russet glow which gilded the table and a balustrade, a promise of rage and blood, it would now belong to me. . . . At least, I would have saved that much. But I was unsuspecting, the ice melted on my tongue, I thought: "Old gold, love, mystical glory." And I lost everything.[44]

This reference would invalidate Sartre's statement concerning the intrinsic significance of qualities, were it not for the ambiguity of the colors concerned, hesitating between red and yellow, the latter color suggesting the permanence of ancient glories while red suggests the unleashing of violent vital urges. Russet, in the following passage, seems to suggest to Mathieu the stability of settled existences: ". . . he was looking at all those flushed faces, those russet moons gliding on small cloud cushions: 'They have lives. . . .' " [45] Russet is the only color which seems to please Roquentin, the historian trying to live in the past: ". . . that beautiful red flame which gilds my head, that's my hair . . . I am glad I am red-headed." [46] Russet rids him of his nausea:

> The room was almost deserted. I had difficulty in recognizing it because I knew I would never come back. It was as light as a vapor, almost unreal, all russet . . . I had the charming impression of penetrating a wood strewn with golden dead leaves.[47]

The explanation of this euphoria follows: "But this wood was so calm, so pure; it seemed to me that it hardly existed and that Nausea had spared it." [48] To Boris, russet connotes the end of a perfect day.[49] It would therefore seem that russet, or orange, conveys to Sartre's characters the stability of that which is solidly anchored in the past, whether it is a life, an antique glory, or the end of day. To all of them, this retreat into the realm of essences is a release from the anxiety of the moment.

Strangely enough, pure yellow seldom appears in Sartrean symbolism. Its meaning is clearly indicated by this brief allusion to Daniel's fascination with the memory of a gaudily lighted penny-arcade or fairground, once the center of his debaucheries: ". . . there was a spot before his eyes, the memory of a thick egg-yellow light: it repelled and attracted him at once. . . ."[50] We infer that yellow symbolizes to Daniel the appeal of a shameful past, its absolute immanence within him. We have here a convergence of yellow and viscosity, and it seems that, through a sort of synesthesia, the yellow and viscous qualities have a similar connotation.

Green seems to hold a privileged place in Sartre's symbolic color scheme. It is Mathieu's favorite color and is frequently associated with the idea of light and of water. Mathieu has just rejected the offer made to him by a former schoolmate to join the Communist party:

> Mathieu looked at his insidious green arm chair, his chairs, his green curtains. . . . The room was no more than a patch of green light that quivered when an autobus passed by. Mathieu went up to the window, and leaned on the balcony. He thought: I *could* not accept, and the room was behind him like calm water. . . .[51]

The symbolic significance of green is associated with that of water in this passage, and is just as ambiguous. It stands between yellow (acceptance of things as they are, objectivity) and blue (transcendent subjectivity). It fits in with the sort of liberty symbolized by water, and is presented here as the intellectual's delight because it connotes at once freedom of action and self-refusal. One may have noticed, in passages quoted above, that to Mathieu green evokes youth, and that "the green and living smell" of summer causes him to wink and smile. The two meanings are not incompatible; youth offers more possibilities of choice than the "age of reason," and Mathieu's youth was dedicated to liberty without commitment. In Gomez the painter, the perception of green takes the form of an urge to recreate life on the plane of art:

> . . . there was that green on the other side of the window-pane, that *natural,* unachieved, ambiguous green, an organic secretion . . . there was that green to be grabbed; I shall attract it, I shall bring it to incandescence. . . .[52]

From the symbolic significance of variations of light, one may infer that whitish light connotes to Sartre a consciousness clouded by its object as the transparency of light may be clouded by particles in suspense. This suggestion is carried by solid white, which seems to stand for the dimness of consciousness caused by the fascination of some external object. Hence, perhaps the sense of catastrophe associated with white by Sartre, as by Melville before him in *Moby Dick*: "Since they glued those white [mobilization] posters on the wall, all lives are failures, all lives are dead." [53]

The admixture of white into any color would seem to dim that color's quality. Pink, for instance, may derive from red its biological connotation, but in a dim, insidious sort of way; as Mathieu enters Marcelle's room, ". . . a rosy mist which smelled of iris fused outside of her room and spread into the stairway. He entered; it always seemed to him that he was entering a shell." [54]

Black stands for the night of consciousness. It may refer to the complete absence of consciousness of being-in-itself, to the "compressed darkness which is the inside of things," [55] or to the self-nihilation of consciousness, its possibility of shutting itself out of a situation, of plunging the world, at least temporarily, into darkness. In that sense, a wink may be described by the waiter in *Huis-clos* (*No Exit*) as "a little black flash" which annihilates the world.[56] It is probably in the same sense that we should interpret Odette's desire to sleep in the "soft black grass," rather than in her husband's car during their flight from Paris at night. When Daniel solicits a sign from the blue, the answer comes from within himself in the form of "an opaque look, night in person," [57] which objectifies him for eternity. The opacity of black implies the night, or obfuscation, of individual consciousness: its loss of transcendence, sense of responsibility, liberty, and anguish, all these burdens being temporarily assumed by the consciousness of others hypostatized under the concept of God.

Both black and white symbolize the opacity of consciousness, with, perhaps, this distinction: black is opacity from within; white from without. The polarity of black and white seems to fascinate Sartre. He praises Audiberti for having mentioned "the secret blackness of milk." [58] These colors are juxtaposed in the magnificent picture of occupied Paris, as seen through Daniel's eyes: "The desert everywhere, tiny chips of palaces hopping here and there, black and white, pigeons, immemorial birds, turned into stones from having fed on statues." [59] Black and white, the quality of stone, converge here to suggest a frozen world, a civilization objectified and petrified by the Medusa look of the victor.

Although their gamut is limited, odors play a decisive part in Sartre's symbolism. The smell of the pines guided Mathieu on the road to freedom:

> Seated in the shadow of the pines, out of breath, his nostrils filled with the smell of rosin, he had had the impression of being an explosion in suspense, throughout the air, round, abrupt, unexplainable. He had said to himself: I shall be free. . . .[60]

This smell retains its value later in his life: "For the first time in a week, he felt at home . . . there was that odor of rosin, and there was that night wind, restless and disquieted, a wandering soul. . . ." [61] As the German army approaches, he realizes that this purposeless liberty will soon be no more than a youthful dream:

> A timid fragrance of absinthe and mint. . . . Green and gay odors, still sharp, still acid; they would become more and more sugary, more and more opulent and feminine, as the sky would turn bluer, as the German half-tracks would come nearer.[62]

Mathieu's values are made clear through this use of synesthesia: "acid" fragrances and green connote the same youthful aspiration toward freedom, while the sweeter, richer fragrances suggest passivity and abandon. The bluer sky remains as the reminder of an inaccessible ideal.

Even more than odors, sounds are more easily evoked through the use of synesthesia. Sartre often joins auditory with tactile sensations better to suggest their symbolic connotations. These may be easily grasped: ". . . an enormous, pasty, heavy detonation had burst in his ear";[63] or they may be rather elusive: "A silky snore startled him. . . ."[64]

As a philosopher, however, Sartre distrusts the use of words for their sounds only, as may occur in poetry. Thus, he turns to ridicule Lucien's delight upon hearing that his state of mind is *"le désarroi"* (disarray): *"Désarroi:* the word had begun tender and white as moonlight, but the final "oi" had the brass glare of a horn."[65] Lucien will one day discover his destiny in the color of his father's eyes: "the grey, metallic and cold eyes of a leader." For the moment, he is enjoying, with his surrealist friends, participating in one of those revolutions which leave the world unchanged, and are therefore well-suited to the false turbulence of conservative youth.

If he disapproves the symbolic use of sound as applied to language, Sartre grants a privileged part to music in the development of two novels. It is through hearing a record of *Some of these days* that Roquentin sees the futility of his escape into the past, and discovers a possible new dimension of time:

He existed, like other people, in the world of public gardens, bistros, industrial cities, and he wished to convince himself that he lived elsewhere, behind the canvases of paintings, with the Doges of Tintoretto, with the brave Florentines of Gozzoli, behind the pages of books. And then, after making quite a fool of himself, he opened his eyes and saw that there had been a wrong deal: he was just in a bistro, behind a glass of tepid beer. He remained crushed on his bench; he thought: "I am a fool." And at that precise moment, on the other side of existence, in that other world which one can see from afar, without ever approaching it, a little melody started to dance, to sing: "It is like me that one must be: one must suffer in rhythm." [66]

The nausea has disappeared. How did it happen? Outside of *our* time, there is another sort of duration: ". . . outside, there is that band of steel, the narrow duration of music, which traverses our time through and through, and rejects it, and tears it apart with its dry little points, there is another time." [67] Music represents another time, because, in musical duration, everything *has to* happen and to happen through design: ". . . nothing can interrupt it, nothing which may come from this time wherein the world lies prostrate; it will cease by itself, by order." [68] As the musical phrase develops and reaches completion, the symbolic gratifying of our expectation imparts the feeling that the ending has been sought and prepared all along in the composer's consciousness. Each note is grounded in consciousness, justified by its participation in a general scheme. What music conveys to Roquentin is the ideal value of being-in-itself-for-itself, the realization of which can only take place on the symbolic plane of art.

The great aria of *Cavalleria Rusticana* would not, however, have permitted Roquentin to realize and to transcend the mediocrity of his whole existence, nor would it have suggested the possibility of suffering in rhythm. To assume and transcend at once the situation, such as it is, is the message imparted by the lyrical transcription of lowly suffering: not to escape into an ideal world, but to bear your existence as if it were a poem of your own composition with the continuity of a musical phrase.

The transcendent—or ecstatic—quality of music is made even more explicit in a somewhat similar passage of *L'Age de Raison,* which describes how Mathieu is enabled to survey his whole existence and judge it, through the suggestion of a "sad and rugged tango":

> . . . suddenly, above his sluggish body, above his life, a pure consciousness began to soar. . . . It was a look glancing at the false bohemian, at the petty bourgeois clinging to his comfort, at the intellectual failure: "not a revolutionist, just a rebel," at the abstract dreamer surrounded by his flabby existence, and it thought: "This fellow is done for, he asked for it. . . ." A red consciousness, a somber little lament: *Mio caballo murio,* it was up to anything, getting truly desperate about the Spaniards, taking a decision. If only it could last that way. . . . But it could not last.[69]

This "purifying ecstasy" is a phenomenon of short duration. Borne on Mathieu's love for Ivich, it implies at once realization of that love and its renunciation. It is "pure reflection" because it assumes that love and does not try to consider it as an abstract Wagnerian "love-in-itself"; Mathieu *is* that love, and he is also the false bohemian, Marcelle's lover. Moments such as these, in which consciousness almost succeeds in cutting itself from the world to glance a total situation, are akin to mystical states; they cannot last.

Tastes have a somewhat similar range of significations as auditory sensations, but they are more often mentioned by Sartre to suggest the apprehension of existence in itself, physiological and dormant, outside of its transcendence: "a little pool of whitish water" to Roquentin,[70] "a stale taste of blood and rusty water" to Mathieu,[71] it is definitely an anti-value to both characters. As one may have observed, sugary tastes are associated with the quality of viscosity, and partiality to them indicates a certain willingness of consciousness to become sluggish and lose its transcendence. On the contrary, acid or sharp tastes are associated with the restlessness of a consciousness in revolt against its "factuality," i.e., the situation which it has to reflect, and are favored by the characters in quest of liberty, even though it be a barren sort of liberty.

To conclude this brief survey of Sartre's literary use of existential symbolism on the plane of perception, let us remark that it is consistent with its philosophical formulation. Whereas, however, the particular meanings of a few symbols such as light, water, and viscosity have been made explicit in *L'Etre et le Néant,* we had to rely on cumulative evidence for the interpretation of other symbols such as colors, perfumes, and tastes. In most cases, the passages quoted above called for an explanation which could only be given on the plane of symbolism.

3. IMAGINATIVE SYMBOLISM

In imagination as in perception, according to Sartre, consciousness *aims* at an object; but in imagination, it aims at an absent object. This object may often have a symbolic meaning. The image is not *in* consciousness, like a faded photograph in the family album: "the image is like an incarnation of non-reflective thought." [72] It figures therefore in Sartre's fiction as the spontaneous apprehension of a situation and of a project, or attitude, concerning that situation, and the meanings of existential symbolism are the same as on the plane of perception.

In *La Chambre,* the flying stone statues which visit Pierre, the madman, correspond to the total loss of consciousness which threatens him: a loss of consciousness which may result from a project of self-annihilation on the part of Pierre's non-reflective consciousness: a return to the opacity and compactness which we have already found symbolized by the "stony" quality on the perceptive plane.

Daniel's pity for Marcel appears to him as "an enormous

slimy pity." [73] The insidious fascination of a misery that does not know itself is indeed about to "swamp" his whole existence. Insofar as he yields to that fascination, to forget his own indignity and get rid of the burden of liberty, we see how the quality of viscosity may be attached to it. Again when he is about to drown his cats, he becomes "filled with stale, viscous water: himself." [74]

Young Lucien's still dim consciousness appears to him as a little fog: "While he was looking at the silverware, he thought that he was looking at the silverware, and, behind that glance, a small living fog was palpitating . . . that fog was himself." [75] Lucien's consciousness is from then on to retain something of that opacity. He has given up the lucidity of subjectivity, and will sooner or later resign himself to live "in the eyes of others."

The ideal value of being-in-itself-for-itself, uniting the transparency of consciousness with the compactness of being, appears to Ivich in the symbolic image of the diamond:

> "I don't care about exams," said Ivich, "I'll be glad if I flunk. Tonight, I bury my bachelor life."
> She smiled and said with an ecstatic air:
> "It shines like a small diamond."
> "What shines like a small diamond?"
> "This moment. It is quite round, it hangs in empty space like a small diamond." [76]

Apparently, thanks to an advanced stage of intoxication, she thinks she has realized the esthete's project of finding the absolute in a perfect moment.

In Mathieu's mind, the transparency of consciousness is evoked by the image of ice: "He attracted her against him; he did not exactly feel any desire for her . . . it was rather the want to see that rebellious and angular spirit melt like a needlepoint icicle in the sun." [77] Mathieu is made aware by this curious image of his own barren liberty and destitute consciousness: "Between those flowers, in the depth of that crevice, a transparency is gliding and contemplating itself with icy passion." [78]

Images sometimes closely follow the perception of objects to which a symbolic interpretation has been attached. Immediately after seeing the sky's azure, Daniel imagines the black look which symbolizes the objectification of his consciousness in the consciousness of others. As he is looking at the Nazi flag, "the standard of bleeding flesh," he imagines that: "a red drop is formed every second within the folds, detaches itself, falls on the macadam: virtue is bleeding." [79] For a short time, this image helps him to drown his feeling of individual guilt in the sense of universal guilt.

Other illustrations could be found to show that, in Sartre, the image merely replaces a missing perception in the joint realization of a situation and of an attitude concerning that situation. A study of the symbolic significance of visions and dreams in his works would probably prove them to be related to patterns of behavior similar to those noted above. Such a study would raise new problems, of a psychological nature, such as (for instance) the nature of madness, which exceed the scope of this essay.

4. CONCLUSION

Existential symbolism is only one of the elements of Sartre's philosophy incorporated in his literary works. Because it comprises the totality of his characters' relations with the things of this world, outside of mere instrumentality, its place in his writings should not be underestimated. It may, in fact, be considered as an extension and illustration of a philosophical conception on the plane of literature. Since there is for Sartre no authentic frame of reference from which to contemplate the world, it is largely a symbolic universe that we discover in his works through disconnected glimpses into the characters' private worlds.

Existential symbolism should, in principle, enable the writer of fiction to relate, directly or indirectly, the most minute perceptions and the most fleeting images within the stream of consciousness of each character to the life-project of that character. Conversely, the reader, in the role of psychoanalyst, should be able to detect, through the reactions of each character to form, color, texture, or odor, what that project is.

To the objection that Sartre's existential symbols do not always speak for themselves, and that their meanings are obvious only to one familiar with the author's philosophy, one may grant that the deciphering of symbols is arduous but insist that it is always rewarding to those who want to go beyond their immediate impressions and the mysterious suggestions words offer on the purely aesthetic plane. This effort is but the price paid for a form of writing deeply and honestly grounded in thought.

Indeed Sartre has opened the way to a new form of symbolism, at once strict in signification, wide in application, and rich in possibilities. Through it he has established a most definite relationship between philosophy and literature.

6

"That Art Thou Not": *Existentialism and Mysticism*

I am not, o my God, what is; alas, I am almost what is not. I see myself as
an incomprehensible intermediate between nothingness and being. I am the
one who has been; I am the one who will be; I am the one who is no
longer what he has been; I am the one who is not yet what he will be; and,
in this in-between that I am, something unknowable that cannot be held in
itself, that has no consistency, that flows away like water; something unknowable that I cannot seize, that flees from my hands, that is no longer
as soon as I wish to grasp or perceive it; something unknowable that finishes
at the very instant in which it begins; so that I can never at any moment
find myself stable and present to myself, so as to simply say that I am. Thus
my duration is nothing but a perpetual swooning.

FÉNELON

I. FROM INTUITION TO MYSTICISM

It is not by chance that the vogue of existentialism
closely followed a wave of mysticism, which had been preceded
by the popularity of philosophies of intuition at the beginning of
this century; these three movements constitute a continuous reaction to the supremacy of pure objective knowledge.

Everyone is familiar with the uneasiness which attends any
attempt to figure out exactly what knowledge *is,* to relate *being*
with *knowing,* or, more generally, with *consciousness.* So long
as we remain in the plane of doing, facing some task related to
some causal sequence, knowing about things appears to us not
only sound but gratifying; but as soon as

> . . . the native hue of resolution
> is sicklied o'er with the pale cast of thought,

as soon as consciousness turns away from the plane of doing to question its own relation with the world of being, the inevitable split takes place within ourselves between object and subject, between the knower and the known. The known always in some way refers to the knower—it is so because *I* know it is so—and the knower to the known: the world around me and my own body testify to the fact of my presence to the world. In William James' words:

> The world of our experience consists at all times of two parts, an objective and a subjective part, of which the former may be incalculably more extensive than the latter, and yet the latter can never be omitted or suppressed.[1]

Our objective knowledge of the universe, as James and Bergson pointed out, does not deal with realities but with symbols of realities. The more we try to grasp realities, the more we are referred to our consciousness of them. Cosmic objects, states James, "So far as the experience yields them, are but ideal pictures of something whose existence we do not inwardly possess but only point at outwardly, while the inner state is our very experience itself."[2] As Bergson showed, objectivity is knowing from outside, symbolically and quantitatively; it is patterned after the laws of causality and is less and less reliable as we pass from matter to life and from life to consciousness. Objective knowledge, in fact, is practical knowledge. It tells how things operate but not *what* they are, nor how we can be conscious *that* they are. It tells us about others insofar as we can assimilate them to things and turn them into psychic objects by claiming that we know what "makes them tick." This kind of knowledge may be successful, on the plane of probability, in dealing with a vast number of people, but hardly with the concrete individual, who may be ap-

plying it to me as I study him and changing his pattern of behavior simply because he refuses to be known.

Since objective knowledge cannot give me an insight into
the ultimate reality of things, of people, or of the world, and
since the world refers me to my consciousness of it as a center
of reference, I may be tempted to adopt the pragmatist's view:
I know that the tree exists because *I* can go around it, and I
know about the existence of the chair because I can sit on it.
And perhaps this is the beginning of wisdom, but of wisdom
related to action. It does not enlighten me about the world or
about the human condition. It tends, however, to lessen in me
the sense of the ultimate reality of the world outside of consciousness. This is why it may lead me to seek the answer to the
riddle of existence on the subjective side, in intuition.

As Bergson pointed out, knowing objectively through signs,
concepts, and quantitative measurements is not the only way to
know. The insect which, to provide nourishment for its brood,
performs on the other insect the delicate operation which keeps
it alive but paralyzed must know something about surgery without having studied anatomy. There must be such a thing as
instinctive knowledge, in which the knower does not differenti-
ate himself from the known, but in some way knows other
creatures intimately and directly, and the operation of life within
them, from inside. May it not be that there is some sort of
organic continuity between the self and the cosmos? Is it not
possible to bring to consciousness what we know subconsciously
about ourselves and the world? Instead of trying to reach reality
through the detachment involved in abstract ideas, could we not
reach it through some sort of inward sympathy, through identification with the object, through fusion of the self and the cosmos?
Or, if our aim is less ambitious, could we not reach a fraction of
reality through intuition? May it not be that consciousness is only
a screen which, instead of reproducing reality, merely blots out
that which does not concern the needs of action, in the same way

as Bergsonian memory merely helps us to forget the past, except for whatever fragment of it is relevant to present needs? Related to instinct, a mere fringe of the *élan vital,* intuition, if it were recaptured in some way by reflection, might become the ground of a more authentic knowledge of ourselves and of the world, a form of knowledge relating the knower and the known, the subject and the object.

James expressed similar ideas on the plane of psychology: "Knowledge about life is one thing; effective occupation of a place in life, with its dynamic currents passing through your being, is another." [3]

> . . . a conscious field *plus* its object as felt or thought of *plus* an attitude towards the object *plus* the sense of a self to whom the attitude belongs—such a concrete bit of personal experience may be a small bit, but it is a solid bit as long as it lasts; not hollow, not a mere abstract element of experience, such as the "object" is when taken all alone. It is a full fact, even though it be an insignificant fact; it is of the *kind* to which all realities whatsoever must belong; the motor currents of the world run through the like of it. . . . [4]

Concrete knowledge of this kind, taking into account subject and object at once, would aim at recovering within ourselves the operation of life, or of the world mind, so that we might *be* what we know. Whatever apprehension of reality we might get through it would be brief, vague, or incomplete, but it would be a more substantial form of knowledge than scientific knowledge could ever be. To quote James again: "A bill of fare with one real raisin on it instead of the word 'raisin'; with one real egg instead of the word 'egg,' might be an inadequate meal, but it would be at least a commencement of reality." [5]

This form of awareness, according to James and Bergson, is related to art and poetry. On the religious plane, it corresponds to what Bergson understands by open religion and James by mysticism. Historically considered, mysticism has never ceased to enlarge, enrich, and vivify other forms of knowledge. As Huxley, after James, repeatedly told us, it can be summed up by three words: *Tat Tvam Asi:* "That art thou." Under various forms, generally derived from Neo-Platonism, but springing from an older Indo-European tradition, it has inspired many more religious leaders, writers, artists, and scientists than is commonly acknowledged; and, not without justification, Bergson finally came to consider it as the positive pole in the dialectical process of progress. Both Newton and Hegel appear to have found in it the suggestion of theories which have contributed to changing our conception of the physical universe and of human society. Most of the romantic philosophers and poets, the New England Transcendentalists, later Romain Rolland, Aldous Huxley, and even Somerset Maugham, have popularized that tradition in western thought, and we can safely state by now that there has never been any interruption in its transmission; it has been at least as influential in shaping western culture as the Judeo-Christian tradition, and may be said to have crept into Christianity itself through various channels. St. Augustine is one of them.

2. THE MYSTICAL APPROACH AND ITS TWO "WAYS"

The Augustinian vision of God *"intimior intimo meo et superior summo meo,"* as deeper in me than my most intimate self, is beyond doubt very close to mysticism. Augustine's stress on subjectivity, exemplified by his anticipation of the Cartesian *cogito* and of the Sartrean pre-reflective *cogito,* does indeed make of him a distant precursor of modern existentialism, but at the same time it establishes a first link between Platonic, and Neo-Platonic, mysticism and a philosophy which would seem, at first glance, to be its very antithesis. Such is the vexing paradox which we will have to face.

The claims of modern Thomism to represent the most authentic form of existentialism further complicate matters. If existentialism can be traced at once to Plato through Augustine, and to Aristotle through Saint Thomas, the term "existentialism" has received such a wide extension that it has ceased to mean anything at all. This question has not been definitely cleared. Yet, the theory of knowledge derived from Plato by the mystics does differ essentially from that derived from Aristotle by the Thomists. Aristotelian knowledge consists in making the knowable object *like* the mind. According to Aristotle, "the same is known by the same"; for a Neo-Platonist like Eckhart, in Otto's words: "Mystical hypertension and exaltation consist in replacing similitude by *identity:* I must be what I know; being and knowledge are identical (a purely mystical axiom)." [6]

In Hinduism likewise, the Atman and Brahman, the individual soul and the soul of the world are one. To quote James again:

> . . . mysticism and the conversion rapture and Vedantism and transcendental idealism bring in their monistic interpretations and tell us that the finite self rejoins the absolute self, for it was always one with God and identical with the soul of the world. [7]

This feeling of identity between the finite self and the absolute self is more or less pronounced according to the mystic; it is seldom pure in the Spanish mystics, it reaches its maximum intensity in Eckhart; not only does he affirm that the soul is one with the eternal Being, but he finds in his own soul a distant memory of Creation: "God created all things through me while I was in the unfathomable depth of God." [8] In our age, Romain Rolland, in his efforts to do away with the problem of evil, came to believe in a God who struggles and suffers within ourselves. Generally speaking, mysticism, at all times and in all places, presents the same claims; and these claims are such as to explain why lack of humility should distinguish the mystic from the purely religious man. *Insofar* as the mystic has succeeded in forgetting his own limited ego in the vision of God, he identifies himself with the eternal creative force. " 'That art Thou!' say the

Upanishads, and the Vedantists add: 'Not a part, not a mode of That, but, identically That, that absolute spirit of the World.' " [9]

To non-mystics, such a statement immediately raises the question: granting that I can identify myself with the creative force of the world, how can I identify myself with the creation itself? How could a mode of knowledge which identifies the knower and the known apply to the objects of the world? To explain the mystic's relative unconcern with this question, it might perhaps help to note that to the mystical mind the world has already lost part or all of its ultimate reality, whether, as in Platonism, things have become the mere shadows of eternal ideas, or, as in the Heraclitean tradition, have been placed between being and non-being as subject to time and change, or, as in Parmenides, denied, by reason of their multiplicity, the truth and reality which belongs only to Unity.

This is how, to the first inward way toward union with a God *intimior intimo meo,* deeper in me than my self, mysticism adds a second way, the outward way: the immediate awareness of God through apprehension of the Unity of a world, the solidity of which has been undermined by absolute subjectivity. To quote Otto on the relationship between the two ways: by the first way:

> . . . I know God only insofar as, and because, I receive my essence from him, which means that I *am* that which I *know*. And this is also the maxim of the knowledge of the second way. Indeed, I only know the All-and-One, the *universum* and the *unum,* as such, because I am all with all, because I am with and in everything, a single and identical thing with the One.[10]

According to Otto, Fichte is representative of the inward path which leads to the contemplation of the Eternal within ourselves, while Hegel is representative of the outward way: "I sacrifice myself to the incommensurable, I am in it, I am the whole, I am nothing but the whole." [11]

Only through such mystical postulates can we understand

the frequently mentioned affinities between mysticism and romanticism. Such postulates indeed are the ground not only of romantic philosophy but of romantic literature as well. Still rather esoteric in the romantic age, they have been made the subject of popular fiction in ours. Somerset Maugham describes in *The Razor's Edge* the two ways of mysticism. The first way, for good reasons, is described from outside:

> He continued to look at me with a strange intensity and then suddenly his body became rigid, his eyes seemed to turn inwards and I saw that he had fallen into the trance which the Indians call Samadhi and in which they hold that the duality of subject and object vanishes and you become Knowledge Absolute.[12]

The second way, somewhat more accessible to the non-mystic, is described from inside as a trance which takes possession of the narrator at the sight of sunrise:

> I was ravished with the beauty of the world. I'd never known such exaltation and such transcendent joy. I had a strange sensation, a tingling that arose in my feet and travelled up to my body and as a pure spirit partook of a loveliness I had never conceived. I had a sense that a knowledge more than human possessed me, so that everything that had been confused was explained. I was so happy that it was pain and I struggled to release myself from it, for I felt that if it lasted a moment longer I should die; and yet it was such rapture that I was ready to die rather than forget it.[13]

It is in this second form, hardly distinguishable from romantic pantheism, that mysticism, from Rousseau to Walt Whitman, has received the widest extension. Yet it is related to mysticism of the first kind historically (through Fénelon's Quietism) as well as psychologically. As Otto says,

> The first and the second ways are . . . similarly characterized by the identification of subject and object. He who sees unity sees himself as one with the One. Now, he who looks inward knows his inward self as one and unified with the divine. Thus in *one as in the other* line, one sees the original duality similarly vanish.[14]

In the mysticism of the second path opposites vanish into unity: in Plotinus, for instance, "the black does not cease being black nor the white being white. But the black is also the white and the white is also the black. Opposites coincide without ceasing being what they are in themselves." [15]

Such is the unifying vision of the mystic: a vision in which subject and object, unity and multiplicity fuse into One True Being; or, if one prefers, an intuition that Being, Unity, and Truth are identical. While gratifying to our logic and craving for simplification, this fusion immediately arouses in us a strong sense of unreality; we cannot do away with the notion of separateness which, in our mind, is inseparable from existence. To this feeling, Huxley has given literary expression in his novel, *Eyeless in Gaza:*

> Reality of unity, but equal reality of division—greater reality, indeed, of division. No need to meditate the fact of division. One is constantly aware of it. Constantly aware of being unique and separate; only sometimes, and then often only intellectually, only as the result of a process of discursive thought, aware of being one with other minds, other lives and all being. Occasionally an intuition of unity, an intuition coming at random, or sought for, step by step, in meditation. . . .
>
> And, of course, if there is to be existence—existence as we know it—being must be organized in closed universes. Minds like ours can only perceive undifferentiated unity as nothing. Unescapable paradox that we should desire that n should be equal to one, but in fact, *we should always find that one is equal to nought.*
>
> Separation, diversity—conditions of our existence. Conditions upon which we possess life and consciousness, know right and wrong and have the power to choose between them, recognize truth, have experience of beauty. But separation is evil. Evil, then, is the condition of life, the condition of being aware, of knowing what is good and beautiful.[16]

The non-mystic indeed can, through discursive thought, conceive Unity as the supreme reality, but he cannot do away with the feeling of separation: separation between things, separation between things and his consciousness of them. This unifying vision in which all separations are abolished he can conceive only as the absence of thought. It seems as if consciousness, about to identify itself with the absolute, fell into pure Non-Being. How can mysticism countenance the phenomenon of Non-Being?

3. MYSTICISM AND NON-BEING

The encounter with Non-Being is indeed a familiar experience for the mystic. According to Zen Buddhism:

> Emptiness constantly falls within our reach, it is always with us and in us, and conditions all our knowledge, all our deeds, and is our life itself. It is only when we attempt to pick it up and hold it forth as something before our eyes that it eludes us, frustrates all our efforts, and vanishes like vapour.[17]

The mystic, it would seem, encounters non-being in God, in the creature and in creation. We should note, however, that this non-being is often charged, so to speak, with some sort of positivity.

He encounters it in God because God can only be defined negatively, like Jaspers' Transcendence: Brahman is neither *this* nor *that* nor anything conceivable; but this negative definition, states James, "is a denial made in behalf of a deeper yes":

> Whoso calls the Absolute anything in particular, or says that it is *this,* seems implicitly to shut it off from being *that*—it is as if he lessened it. So we deny the "this" negating the negation which it seems to imply, in the interests of the higher affirmative attitude by which we are possessed.[18]

To Dionysius the Areopagite:

> The cause of all things is neither soul nor intellect; nor has it imagination, opinion, or reason, or intelligence; nor is it reason, or intelligence; nor is it spoken or thought. It is neither number, nor order, nor magnitude, nor littleness, nor equality, nor inequality, nor similarity. It neither stands, nor moves, nor rests. . . . It is neither essence, nor eternity, nor time. . . .[19]

Böhme writes of Primal Love that "it may fitly be compared to Nothing, for it is deeper than any Thing, and is as nothing in respect to all things, for as much as it is not comprehensible by any of them. And because it is nothing respectively, it is therefore free from all things. . . ."[20]

This kind of "negative theology" leads Eckhart to make his distinction between God and the original Deity, "where never was seen difference, neither Father, Son, nor Holy Ghost, where there is no one at home, yet where the spark of the soul is more at home than in itself."[21] In Eckhart indeed, the Deity, as undifferentiated totality, comes close to absolute Non-Being, yet we must presume that it is also Absolute Being.

Since, in all forms of mysticism, the Self or individual soul tends to identify itself with the Divine Soul, its definition curiously varies from absolute nothingness to participation in the Absolute Being of God. As in popular usage the very word "creature" implies depreciation. To Eckhart, for instance, "All creatures are pure non-being."[22] This pure non-being remains an enigma since the creature "exists" with its non-being. In Çankara the creature is a product of Avidyâ, the veil of multiplicity and error, for Plotinus, "the creature holds its non-being from matter."[23] Through "purgation" the mystic rids himself of his nothingness. He is *insofar* as he participates in God's being. Again we shall resort to Somerset Maugham for a familiar illustration of this theme:

> "You talk very familiarly of the Absolute, Larry, and it's an imposing word. What does it actually signify to you?"
>
> "Reality. You can't say what it is; you can only say what it isn't. It's inexpressible. The Indians call it Brahman. It's nowhere and everywhere. All things imply and depend upon it. It's not a person, it's not a thing, it's not a cause. It has no qualities. It transcends permanence and change; whole and part, finite and infinite. It is eternal because its completeness and perfection are unrelated to time. It is truth and freedom.
>
> ". . . But how can a purely intellectual conception be a

solace to the suffering human race? Men have always wanted a personal God to whom they can turn in their distress for comfort and encouragement."

"It may be that at some far distant day greater insight will show them that the need to worship is no more than the survival of an old remembrance of cruel Gods that had to be propitiated. I believe that God is within me or nowhere. . . ."[24]

While the Absolute defined in this passage evokes *The One* of Plotinus, a superessential Non-Being which is the source of all being, we might note in passing that it bears a curious resemblance to Sartre's Non-Being, neither *this,* nor *that,* nor anything imaginable, the source of truth and freedom, within me or nowhere. Let us simply conclude, for the moment, that God's creature in mysticism tends to be either nothing or an absolute according to whether or not it participates in the being of God, who alone *Is.*

The creation undergoes in the mystic's mind the same depreciation or, according to the case, the same glorification, as the creature, but we might make bold to suggest that it does so with a certain amount of ambiguity. No doubt, to Çankara, the world of things in their multiplicity can only be through Avidyâ, the veil of illusion and wrong thinking, but if it is a pure being, how can it coexist with Brahman, who alone *Is,* and if not, how can it generate the world in its diversity? Therefore, "Avidyâ (and similarly the multiplicity generated by Avidyâ) can be designated neither as being nor as non-being."[25] In the same way, Eckhart states that "Nothing created has reality in itself."[26] Yet neither Eckhart nor Çankara are subjective idealists. The world to them is not simply "my representation." It *is* truly, but only in unity, as the Eternal One. To prove the ultimate reality of things perceived, Çankara uses an argument which vaguely reminds us of Sartre's introductory quest of being in *Being and Nothingness:* "Either it is the very being of A or else it is the A-being of A which is the object of perception. Now it is impossible that it be the second, for it presupposes the first to be itself possible." [27] In other words, the being of the object as object refers to Being pure and simple. Whether dealing with God, the creature, or the world, mysticism always refers us to a Being which is Truth and Unity, without really explaining its multiplicity and the evil of separateness. As in the poetry of Marguerite de Navarre, the veil of Avidyâ is expected to recede before the unifying vision of the mystic, as darkness has to recede before light. It is a question of perceiving the many in the One, as in romantic pantheism; but the romanticist's ecstasy often leads him to the vision of a degraded or non-existent world. Such is the case in Rousseau's celebrated *Cinquième Rêverie,* or in this description of a jonquil, quoted by James, in *The Varieties of Religious Experience,* from Senancour's *Obermann:*

> It was the strongest expression of desire: it was the first perfume of the year. I felt all the happiness destined for man. This unutterable harmony of souls, the phantom of an ideal world arose in me complete. I never felt anything so great or so instantaneous. I know not what shape, what analogy, what secret of relation it was that made me see in this flower a limitless beauty . . . I shall never inclose in a conception this power, this immensity that nothing can express; this form that nothing can contain; this ideal of a better world which one feels, but which, it seems, nature has not made actual. . . .[28]

James fails to point out clearly that the harmonious world embodied, as an intention of nature, by the flower, is in fact given as inexistent. Blake, with his "Tyger," and before him the disciples of Socrates, had already suspected that the deciphering of symbols does not lead to the vision of a unified, harmonious world. A by-product of romantic Platonism, Symbolism rather tends, in Poe and Baudelaire, to the conception of a world degraded from its very inception by the passage from Unity to Duality. While obviously, as James and Bergson contend, philosophy has much to learn from mysticism, it cannot resign itself either to seeking Unity by escaping from the world through the nirvana of blank contemplation, or to seeking in the world

itself a unity which only appears as an ideal value, to be denied
by concrete experience.

Romantic mysticism led to Hegel's philosophy of "mediation." "In its depth," states a Hegel scholar, "Hegel's philosophy
is a reflection upon a mystical experience." [29] From a poem
written in his youth, Hegel crossed out the following lines:

> Mind loses itself in extasy;
> What I called "mine" vanishes;
> I surrender to the incommensurable,
> To it I belong, I am the All, the All only.
> Reason, recaptured, is estranged;
> Thrilling before infinity, stupefied,
> It does not grasp the depth of that extasy. [30]

He crossed out those lines because he had realized that "This
summit of contemplation, in which all oppositions are suppressed could not become a realization in the very absence of
thought." [31] Subjectivity had in some way to be reconciled with
objectivity. Still a mystical postulate underlies Hegelian thought:
the romantic notion of *Identität;* identity of the self with the
soul of the world, with the cosmos itself. Our finite minds participate in the Infinite Mind actualizing itself. Being all parts of
reality, the Infinite Mind can mediate between them. "The opposition of two beings—opposition is distinguished from difference by the fact that the two opposites participate in the same
organic totality—appears only on the condition of presupposing
their unity." [32]

Hegelian dialectics represents an attempt to organize the
clashing elements and the contradictions of the mystical outlook
into an articulate, dynamic form of thought. As in mysticism,
the idea of Being is necessarily characterized by its lack of determination and leads to the idea of Non-Being. But this passage
from Being, as thought, to Non-Being is also, as "objective

idealism," the basis of Hegel's metaphysics. As in Heraclites, so in Hegel, there is nothing in heaven or on earth that does not contain Being and Non-Being. The relation between the two is Becoming. Becoming is the passage of infinity into the finite. The finite becomes finite only through being contrasted with infinity; the finite object, in the same way, contains its relation to that which is not the object. It is finite not because it is limited but because non-being is its nature; it only exists in relation to other things, to pass away into other things. Out of the Heraclitean notion of flux, Hegel derives a new dynamic self-propelled logic in which non-being as negation acquires a sort of positive force.

Just as the opposition of two beings can take place only upon the condition of presupposing their unity, in the same way Being, as a synthesis of subject and object, "has no meaning except in relation to knowledge; hence the position of those who make of it a separate reality is as dangerous as it is absurd." [33] While it tries to be at once subjective and objective, Hegelianism does not surrender the mystical postulates of mysticism. As "objective Idealism," it might be said to be a sort of articulate mysticism; yet it is, paradoxically, one of the sources, if not the main source, of modern existentialism.

Any one who tries to understand Kierkegaard or Sartre in the light of plain Aristotelian logic, according to which a thing either is or is not, is immediately challenged by what seems to be a systematic violation of this principle. Historically, existentialism is given as having sprung from a reaction to the Hegelian "system" in which the truth of anything is in its relation to the totality; but, even when criticizing Hegel most severely, the existentialists seem to be largely influenced by his way of thinking; in Helmut Kuhn's terms, "Kierkegaard's thought might be styled an anti-Hegelianism, and this paradoxical description applies also to most of twentieth-century existentialism." [34]

This is particularly true of Sartre, whose dialectics seems

to be heavily indebted to Hegel's *Phenomenology of the Mind*. What both Kierkegaard and Sartre object to in Hegel is his claim to look at things from the point of view of the totality. Kierkegaard, with his attempt to find truth in subjective intensity, and Sartre, with his return to the *cogito,* maintain that the point of view of the individual self, the point of view of the Here and Now, is the only legitimate point of departure. In a very simplified way, one might say that Sartre represents Hegel thought over from the standpoint of Descartes.

This does not mean that Sartre's philosophy of existence owes nothing to Bergson's philosophy of life, which it continues in some ways. In fact, it appears more and more doubtful whether the philosophy of existence could have become as popular as it did if the philosophy of life had not cleared the way by challenging the pseudo-scientific application of materialistic determinism to the realm of consciousness; but, after all, the sort of freedom which Bergson wanted to restore was patterned after a biological exemplar, being merely a persistence, a preservation of given states of consciousness or, from a more general standpoint, the blind striving of creative evolution. From the level of things, Bergson had merely raised "states of consciousness" to the level of Life, and the fact that conscious life was life operating through inorganic matter did not improve matters much. Whether or not Bergson's philosophy allowed for the negating power of consciousness, the very idea of Non-Being remained for him a pseudo-idea. Something had to be done to restore to the philosophy of intuition and liberty a sort of romantic rationality which alone Hegel through Kierkegaard could offer. The rediscovery of Kierkegaard was contemporary with the wave of mysticism mentioned above, a wave of mysticism which had finally fused with the philosophy of life in Bergson's *Two Sources of Morality and Religion*.

We have so far tried to show that historically, through the philosophy of creative evolution, through the mystical trend in contemporary thought, and through the rediscovery of Kierke-gaard, existentialism was bound to rest on the presupposition of mystical postulates, no matter how imperfectly recognized. Our next, and boldest endeavor will be to detect these postulates in existence philosophies, and particularly in Sartre's existentialism, which seems to be the furthest removed from mystical thought.

5. EXISTENTIALISM VS MYSTICISM: "THAT ART THOU NOT"

Existentialism is not mysticism; yet, if philosophy had never borrowed some of the assumptions of mysticism, it could not have found its way to existentialism. This is true whether or not we reserve to Sartre the title of existentialist, which other existence philosophers do not seem eager to share with him.

Sartre's existentialism is known to be atheistic, in fact has been characterized as "postulatory atheism." [35] The term "mystical atheism," which has also been applied to him is perhaps more exact. To clarify this question, we should first of all note that in all philosophies of existence a clear distinction is made in the notion, or direct intuition, of God: as First Person, directly identified with the subject in the mystic's highest and rarest rapture; as Second Person, i.e., as the Other and Absolute Subject; or as the wholly separate Third Person and Absolute Object —in other words as *I, Thou,* or *He.*

The philosopher of existence stops short of ever thinking of God in the first person, as *I,* like Eckhart, or of identifying the Atman with Brahman, like Çankara. God in the third person appears only to be rejected, except for syntactic necessity. All religious philosophers of existence think of God in the second person. To Kierkegaard, God is not an object, he is an *alter ego,* an absolute subject, a *Thou.* Jasper's Transcendence is what can never become an object; it is neither an individual God, separate from a created world, nor the whole becoming world, nor the God of revelation. Marcel is even more specific: the object we have is *it; it* is the original third person. To treat the other person, or God, as third person is to treat them as objects. The *I* is the subject; yet it is always related to a *Thou,* although we have to separate them for the sake of clarity. God is the *Absolute Thou.* The *Thou* is implied in commitment and it is to the *Absolute Thou* that I am primarily committed. "The less available for commitment I am, the more God appears as *someone who,*" i.e., as a third person.[36] A similar distinction is the very basis of Buber's philosophy: for Buber there are only two planes of existence: the *I-Thou* and the *I-It* planes. The *I-Thou* relation is realization: I realize that I distinguish myself from the other Self, to whom I am related. The *Thou* may also be God, and (this is the second approach of mysticism) the world. The *I-It* relationship is orientation or utilization, a plane on which I treat not only things but other beings and God as objects, or tools. Berdyaev's "personalism," somewhat less specific, nevertheless involves a dialectics of the human and of the Divine, and constitutes a strong rebellion against the common concept of God as wholly separate. "Separation from God makes the world heavy, and heaviness signifies . . . the absence of God."[37] Contact, rather than identification, seems to be the religious existentialist relation with God: "In the depth of his spirituality man finds himself in contact with the divine, and it is from the source of the divine that he receives his support."[38] Like Buber, Berdyaev is opposed to any attempt to objectify the human "personality": "In the process of its self-realization personality ought to carry on a campaign against the objectification which enslaves it. . . ."[39]

Clearly then, all "religious existentialists" agree in their denial of a separate, third person, objectified God. Hence their conciliatory attitude toward atheism which they consider as participating in the campaign against God objectified: "The God that atheism denies, states Marcel, is indeed essentially *someone who.*"[40] Berdyaev goes further and sees in atheism "a dialectical moment in the knowledge of God."[41] "What, in suffering man, stands against God in the name of man is nothing else than the revolt of the true God himself. Revolt against God can take place only in the name of God himself, in the name of a higher idea of God." [42] This explains, incidentally, how "religious existentialists," like Marcel and Berdyaev, can share a common philosophy with Nietzche and Sartre. The God with whom Sartre seems to have a personal quarrel is precisely the impersonal Other objectified; by the "impersonal Other" we must understand that interchangeable and inexistent human being whom we call "one," "they," "people," and whom Heidegger calls *das man;* it is everywhere and nowhere, it is deeper in me than myself, like Augustine's God, but as *not being myself,* and its voice, says Heidegger, is the voice of *das man* in me, a form of inauthentic consciousness. At the same time it is objectified insofar as it is a third person God wholly separate from me and to be propitiated, therefore utilized to my own interest. The objections religious existentialists have against Sartre's atheism is not so much his reviling a distorted notion of God as the delight he seems to take in this negative attitude and his refusal to go beyond the negative moment. Of his attitude toward an objectified God, one might say what his disciple, Simone de Beauvoir, says of his attitude toward society; that he found society such as it is detestable, but did not detest detesting it. [43] Hence the sort of shadow boxing we find in *The Flies,* where he brings to life the sinister figure of Jupiter for the mere pleasure of abusing it. While religious philosophies of existence reject the idea of an objectified and separate God, they still retain in their conception of God a certain mysterious otherness, although this otherness may be part of a structure, as in Buber's *I-Thou* relationship, or a dialectical process as in Berdyaev; they reject the purely mystical notion of an individual self which could fuse with the absolute Self, the prevalent monism of Indian philosophy, to which the existence of a separate soul is an illusion. It is not our purpose here to define the rather elusive *I-Thou* relationship which imparts to religious existentialism its specific character;

suffice it to state that while very close to mysticism, religious existentialism stops short of absolute reliance on the individual self as identical with the absolute Self.

The purpose and scope of Sartre's *Phenomenological Ontology* would seem to preclude any speculations of a metaphysical character; yet in some ways it calls for them. One might go further and say that Sartre's philosophy calls for mystical presuppositions. While rejecting the notion of a separate third person God, which he identifies with the depersonalized Other, Sartre retains that of a God who would, as absolute value, represent the ideal of any human project, and toward whom all human actions would be oriented, until consciousness undergoes a "purifying ecstasy" which he does not clearly define. This ideal is given as an impossibility, but individual consciousness remains, and takes the place of Hegel's Absolute Spirit, facing the task of actualization. Consciousness becomes an absolute, the only absolute, facing the scandal of other consciousnesses, also absolute and therefore incompatible. Yet, like Huxley's hero in *Eyeless in Gaza,* Sartre wonders whether this scandalous multiplicity of absolutes does not refer to an original unity of Mind, similar to Hegel's Absolute Spirit. Indeed, since, according to Sartre, the separation between consciousnesses is the expression of an internal negation, since, in other words, the other first appears to me as a subject, i.e., as an absolute center of reference, since my being for others is a dimension of my being, since I have to deny that I am the other in order to be myself, the relation between my consciousness and the consciousness of others would seem to be one of *identity denied*: ". . . my ipseity (selfness) and that of others are structures of the same totality of being. Thus Hegel seems to be right: it is the point of view of the totality which is the point of view of being, the true point of view." [44] We might then conceive individual consciousness as participating in a totality of world consciousness. On the other hand, however, while my consciousness denies being the other's consciousness, the other's consciousness simultaneously denies being my own. There cannot be individual consciousnesses without the separateness implied by these simultaneous negations. While these negations refer to an original totality of mind, it seems as if non-being "had crept into that totality to break it up, as non-being in Leucippus' atomism creeps into the Parmenidean totality of being to make it burst into atoms." [45] Non-being is not the origin of that multiplicity but it is its expression. Sartre leaves us with the contradictory notion of a totality of mind which not only is "detotalized" but which appears to us like a broken being of which you can neither say that it exists nor that it does not exist." [46]

Could we not resolve the contradiction from a superior standpoint? Sartre claims that we cannot view the totality from outside; neither can we imagine that it could be resolved in God. If God is consciousness, that consciousness must be integrated with the totality (as, we take it, the *élan vital* in creative evolution). "And if, by his nature, He is a being *beyond consciousness,* i.e., a being-in-itself who would be his own foundation, totality can only appear to him as *object.* . . ." [47] This last hypothesis has already been refuted by Sartre. The first would lead us back to the conception of a broken-up totality of consciousness struggling to realize being-in-itself-and-for-itself, and dedicated to failure: "Everything happens as if the world, man and man-in-the-world only succeeded in realizing a God that failed (*un Dieu manqué*)." [48] All in all, it is in individual consciousness that Sartre finds the absolute which the mystic seeks in a transcendental Self; to that extent, he may rightly be accused of deifying man. On the other hand, human consciousness sacrifices itself to a single fundamental value which is the realization of an impossible God. In spite of the inconclusive character of Sartre's metaphysical perspective his *Dieu manqué* is not without similarity to the "fallen God" of late romanticism: a God who is at once our own eager postulation and what is left of the Divine heart: ". . . that Divine heart—What is it? *It is* our own heart," says Poe in *Eureka.* We do not claim that this is Sartre's own unexpressed conclusion; we are merely suggesting that the "scandal" of a multiplicity of consciousnesses can only be a scandal to the unifying vision of the mystic; that his notion of consciousness as neither *this* nor *that,* nor anything imaginable, an absolute Non-Being, yet a Non-Being which is the source of all possibility, is strangely akin to the Hindu conception of Brahman; that his metaphysical conclusions lead him to the gate of a mystery which calls to mind the romantic vision of a fallen God within a fallen world. Of course this is a gate that Sartre would not pass, and it is not without reason that he has been called a romantic rationalist. We shall find further elucidation of his brand of romanticism in his apprehension of the world, as compared with the second way of mystical approach to the unity of Being.

Just as romantic presuppositions may help us to understand—on the plane of negation—the relations between one consciousness and another, they may help us to grasp the relations of consciousness to the world. Fundamentally, consciousness is an absolute negation of identity with whatever it reflects, i.e., the whole world. In rare moments of pantheistic ecstasy, romanticists like Rousseau thought they identified themselves with the world; what really happened was that, facing the world as totality, their consciousness had passed from a negation of *this* or *that* to absolute negation. *This* and *that,* as forms, had merged into the background, generating a sense of unity and the illusion of progressive absorption, generalized fascination. This sort of cosmic consciousness engendered the feeling of a fusion between object and subject insofar as all external negations, or distinctions between *this* and *that,* had vanished; but the negation of identity was still there, between the world as background and consciousness itself. We may note, to support Sartre's contention, that in the descriptions of such ecstatic moments consciousness is not long in reasserting itself in painful realization of their fleeting character. Thus Sartre would seem to have disposed of the second way of mystical knowledge; yet, on the other hand, if consciousness remains "identity denied" as it faces the world, does not this presuppose a mysterious *Identität* of the self and of the cosmos?

The illusion of pantheistic fusion with the world is better understood when we realize that ordinarily consciousness, an absolute negation, makes itself a "qualified negation" by aiming at *this,* or *that,* and making it stand as *form* against a *background.* In this operation, the object is allowed to appear such as it is, while its background fades out into a sort of non-being; but consciousness still remains distinct, as qualifying negation of identity, from what it unveils; and what it unveils is not consciousness but being. Consciousness as "unveiling" reminds us vaguely of Avidyâ, the veil of multiplicity and error; but Avidyâ is constitutive of the world as illusion while consciousness, with Sartre, represents the irruption of Non-Being into the world of Being. This would seem to dispose again of the mystical identification of object and subject. Yet, as in Çankara, the being of *A* calls for Being as such,[49] or to use Sartre's terms, the being of the phenomenon calls for the phenomenon of Being. Being is conferred by consciousness, which in its turn calls for the trans-phenomenal dimension of the object. The same "phenomenon of Being" would seem to be shared by consciousness and its object, and not merely on the plane of knowledge since, as Sartre tells us, we experience being directly in such experiences as nausea and boredom.

The "phenomenon of Being," however, should, in our opinion, reveal pure Being, and not that being which, according to Sartre, already has its non-being coiled in its heart like a worm. It should refer to that undifferentiated Being, which he postulates in his metaphysical perspectives as the original Being, and not to the being of the object; neither could it refer to the sense of being which we experience in nausea. Or rather, if occasionally, it is the whole world of being which appears to us as a meaningless morass, as it does to the hero of *Nausea,* it should be because the being in question is already a mixture of being and non-being. To use Heidegger's terminology, which Sartre does not follow, we are dealing here, not with *das Sein* but with *das Seinde,* which term, being untranslatable in English, might be rendered by "determinate being," or even perhaps "becoming," a becoming, in this case, which has ceased to become, a purely repetitive becoming.

Again we would be confronted, then, with the notion of Being which does not refer to the being of *this,* or *that,* but to Being as such which, in its lack of differentiation, resembles the Being, One and True, of the mystics and can hardly be distinguished, according to Sartre, from Non-Being, the realm of consciousness. If we recall that, for Sartre, Non-Being could only proceed from Being, we are again on the threshold of what Marcel, or even Heidegger with all his reticence, concedes to be the domain of mystery. Nor is this notion of mystery completely missing in Sartre; it appears under the guise of some original and absurd contingency: *it is so because it is so.* Being appears to consciousness such as it is, and if the object has reality for consciousness beyond the succession of its appearances, it is because the series of these appearances can never be exhausted.

Since consciousness is free, in the very act of perception, to "unveil" *this* or *that* object, or quality of the object, perhaps Sartre's analysis of the motivation for this choice might enlighten us on the relations of consciousness to its object: the conjunction of being and non-being. The objects of the world are unveiled to us, either by reason of their practical value (for the use we may make of them in the realization of our projects), or by reason of their symbolic value, as their qualities suggest to us modes of being that conform to these projects.

In the first case, as we recall, the world is simply a tool-complex. Objects suggest to us, on the plane of doing, what we can do with them. This view is not dissimilar to the Bergsonian conception of the world as the sum total of all patterns of behavior offered to *homo faber* for his liberation from the determinism of matter, and through him to the *élan vital* of creative evolution. For Sartre, however, such patterns present themselves as the possible realizations of individual projects related to achievement of certain ways of being: the mountain is to be climbed because climbing mountains fits in with what I have decided to do with myself. The variety of human projects stems, if our interpretation is correct, from the radical impossibility of realizing a fundamental human project which is to ground being in consciousness: to be God. Again, we must note that with Sartre stress is placed on human consciousness as the origin of all values rather than on a cosmic force or absolute spirit.

If we now turn to the symbolic meaning of things, we face a more mysterious world in which every possible quality of form, texture, color, sound and fragrance not only suggests but presents to consciousness certain modes of being. There can be no mistake on that point: everything happens as if the viscosity we encounter in certain patterns of behavior was the same viscosity which repels or attracts us in glue or honey. The arresting fact is not that light (pure consciousness) or water (freedom through change) may attract those who seek pure consciousness or freedom through change but that the unknown structure of material elements may actually be identified with human projects and that Sartre may mention the possibility of a "psychoanalysis of matter." Again this conforms strictly to the tradition of mystical symbolism that we find in Boehme or Swedenborg. Of course, we realize that in Sartre the modes of being remain inaccessible, except on the symbolic plane of appropriation. Nevertheless, Sartre's "as if" philosophy brings us here to the gate of a new kind of mystery, which is no longer the mystery of Being undifferentiated and readily converted into Non-Being, but the very mystery of "being in itself," no longer opaque but fundamentally identical to that consciousness which is its negation: *That art thou not.*

6. CONCLUSION AND POSTSCRIPT

Considering Sartre's ontology from a standpoint strictly opposed to his, and doing the utmost violence to the spirit of his method, starting from the mystical postulate of the identity of Being, Unity, and Truth, to reach down to the intrinsic meanings of differentiated being in its commonplace manifestations, we found that this postulate could figure as a presupposition to the most challenging elements in his dialectics of Being and Non-Being; we found, furthermore, that his analysis had, at least to a degree, elucidated and rationalized the contradictions inherent to mysticism: as in mysticism, so in Sartre, we found the answer to the problem of knowledge in the fundamental identity of subject and object, and this answer was connected with the fundamental identity, so often suggested by mysticism, of Being and Non-Being; but in all cases the identity in question was an identity denied.

The fact that it is denied adds literally *nothing* to it; but that nothingness, if we accept the paradox involved, makes all the difference in the world. Acting as negation, it allows us to see more clearly into the mystery of knowing, to reject at once the excessive claims, first, of objective knowledge, which leaves us completely outside of what we know, without explaining what knowing is and, second, of an intuition that identifies the knower and the known without explaining how the knower can remain distinct from the known. There is no denying that, on the humanistic plane, Sartre's analyses throw a great deal of light, sometimes an almost offensive glare, on human behavior.

But on the other hand, there is no denying either that the candid reader remains puzzled by what, to many critics, appears to be a new kind of Cartesian dualism: the dualism of being-in-itself and being-for-itself, basically of being and non-being. We lack in Sartre a metaphysical dimension which would resolve this opposition, were it only in the most hypothetical way. Sartre indeed attempted such a resolution in the "as if" philosophy of his metaphysical perspectives; but his metaphysics either remains inconclusive or does violence to his phenomenology. He left the door open to someone else for that supreme philosopher's commitment which we call metaphysics, and perhaps for good reasons; for, if our interpretation is correct, it might have led him to some sort of modified, and secularized, mysticism.

"I have nothing against mysticism," Sartre confided to me, "except its belief in a unity which does not exist." This statement would seem to conform rather literally to the metaphysical background which we have been trying to detect in his phenomenology: "Everything happens as if the world, man, and man-in-the-world succeeded only in realizing *un Dieu manqué.*"

Since the preceding analysis was written, several studies have appeared, which should be mentioned here in postscript as confirming the relations of existentialism to mysticism and throwing further light on some aspects of these relations. Henry Nelson Wieman, in "The Problem of Mysticism," admits that while existentialists are not mystics, "the very experiences they describe have a certain bearing on the mystical."[50] The relation of the *I* to the *Thou,* in Buber for instance, appears to him closer than as presented here. As to Sartre, his description of the external world in *Nausea:* "Had I dreamed this enormous presence? It was there, in all the garden, toppled down into the trees, all soft, sticky, soiling everything, a jelly . . ."[51] appears to him as "mysticism at the first stage of transformation," a transformation which, in this case, did not occur. The same passage is associated by Newton T. Stallknecht, in "Mysticism and Existentialism," to the mystic's "dark night of the soul," which generally precedes "a communion with God or Nature which the existentialist is less likely to achieve."[52]

Some interesting comparisons have been made between Sartrean existentialism and the ethical mysticism professed by Albert Schweitzer. By family tradition, states J. Hutton Hind, in "Mysticism and Ethics," Schweitzer belonged to a sect of Christian mysticism tending to consider Christ as a symbol, suggesting a certain quality of spirit: "Schweitzer wished to surrender his own spirit to this 'Holy Spirit.'" [53] Yet, while he felt with certainty that "every thought which thinks itself necessarily ends in mysticism," [54] Schweitzer had an equally strong conviction that his mysticism should take the form of commitment. Henry Babel claims that this philosophy of commitment has rightly been called a form of existentialism. Comparing Schweitzer's commitment to a "reverence for life" and Sartre's self-determined commitment, he concludes that these two forms of commitment are incompatible. [55]

Brought up exclusively by his Schweitzer relatives, Sartre must have been familiar with their tradition in matters of religion; in the short autobiography of his childhood which he recently published, [56] the name of the "Holy Spirit" frequently comes back in the speeches of his grandfather Schweitzer. Stress on the Holy Spirit, and on his kingdom to come, has always marked a certain Christian mysticism of the most intellectual kind. Through Abelard's "Paraclet" to Malebranche's "Vision in God" and pre-romantic occultism, this trend has persisted to our day, mostly in its secularized form. In the opinion of Stallknecht:

> Sartre's philosophy might be compared . . . in quasi-trinitarian terms to a revolt of the Spirit who refuses to admit any dependence upon the Father or Son. From the Father proceeds creative power, but the Spirit is free only in so far as it creates for itself. The Son embodies the wisdom and the way of life, eternally begotten by the Father. But the Spirit can only profit by wisdom that it has itself derived from experience. It can gain nothing by asking assistance. It must help itself. The world may present the human Spirit with problems and difficulties. It may supply the occasion for action. But the decision and the action belongs wholly to the Spirit itself. [57]

Sartre has placed himself outside of the Christian tradition; but belief in a Unity of Mind, accessible to the individual mind, has persisted outside of that tradition, in the *Esprit pur* of Vigny's romantic poetry, for instance, or in the "psychic continuum" of Jules Romains' "unanimism." While not a Christian himself, Romains was much impressed by the fact that sin against the Spirit should have been declared the most unforgivable sin. If Sartre's existentialism constitutes a reaction against mysticism, it is not against the aesthetic type of Platonic mysticism which we encounter in Poe or Baudelaire. This he ignores altogether. In his criticism of Baudelaire, as well as in his criticism of Giraudoux, Sartre fails to distinguish between Aristotelian and Platonic essences. When referring to Platonism, he is thinking of some sort of "intelligible heaven" indeed, but not of the transcendental Ideas suggested by the perception of beauty on earth so commonly alluded to in Renaissance or romantic poetry. The mystical postulates which we undertook to detect in Sartre's humanism are primarily those of intellectual mysticism. Sartre's "identity denied" is first and foremost the identity of the individual mind with a hypothetical World Mind. Intuition of world Unity through the senses or the emotion he does not have to deny because, even in the most fleeting way, it is completely outside of his experience.

To state that Sartre, so often referred to as the archetype of the intellectual, denies the postulate of an identity of Mind, so typical of the intellectual mystic, does not mean that his own intellectual passion is unrelated to that postulate, but that the relation is one of negation, or if one prefers, of rejection. Sartre's so-called "inverted Christianity" would then be, on the philosophical plane, a sort of inverted intellectual mysticism. Sartre himself, in his autobiography, admits that it took him more than thirty years to get rid of his belief in "essences" and that he was not sure of having been completely successful. Belief in essences is not mysticism; but if, as Schweitzer claims, every thought which thinks itself ends in mysticism (or, as Huxley claims, the sense of Unity is reached most often through discursive thought), a determined humanist may find himself having to adopt, if only to reject, the postulates of mysticism, particularly if they form the background of a philosophical tradition which he wants to transfer and establish on the humanistic plane. It is with such postulates, the basic identity of Unity, Truth, and Being, of subject and object, and in the most hypothetical way, of Being and Non-Being, that we have been concerned here, not with the ineffable character of certain mystical experiences, or of whatever bliss may have been derived from them.

On the humanistic plane then, and in spite of the limitations inseparable from the concept of situation, a certain mystical background in existential philosophy may help us to understand how Sartrean consciousness may represent the irruption into the world of being of an absolute Non-Being; how consciousness can in fact constitute an absolute center of reference for the totalitarian organization of the world; how the scandal of multiplicity of consciousnesses may arise from the coexistence of two absolutes; how, finally, each consciousness should be responsible for the whole world, as if it had created the world while it was one with the super-essential Being, source of all being and of its own non-being.

7

Existentialism and Marxism

By placing dialectics back on its feet, Marx revealed the real contradictions
of realism.

Critique de la raison dialectique

Two critical studies in book form have already been
published in this country on the subject of Sartre's Marxism, as
defined in the *Critique de la raison dialectique*. I shall refer to
them extensively in this essay, the only purpose of which is to
relate Sartrean Marxism to the philosophy of *L'Etre et le Néant*,
considered in the light of the preceding essays.

As he declared his allegiance to Marxism in *Critique de la
raison dialectique*, Sartre disavowed none of the objections raised
against Marxist theory in "Matérialisme et Révolution." [1] These
were directed, not only at modern Marxism, which Sartre considers completely ossified, but also at the inconsistencies of original Marxism. The only concession which might indicate a change
of heart on Sartre's part is his suggestion that Marxism is wrong
only in its theory of knowledge. [2] The first subject of dissent was
Marx and Engeles' proclaimed "materialism."

I. MATERIALISM

Marxism professes to be a non-metaphysical form of materialism. According to Sartre, materialism, which reduces the
movements of the mind to those of matter, is a form of meta-

physics insofar as it constitutes an *a priori* hypothesis concerning the universe as totality; yet Marxists refuse to defend their position on metaphysical grounds, and take refuge in a new sort of positivism. Their materialism, they say, is the expression of a progressive discovery of the interaction of physical forces in the world, a discovery which is not passive but implies the activity of the discoverer. Thus the materialist denies subjectivity, becomes himself an object, the matter for scientific knowledge. But once he has suppressed subjectivity, instead of seeing himself as a thing among things, he starts considering himself as a pure objective look and claims to contemplate the world as it is. Having gone beyond all subjectivity and assimilated himself to pure objective truth, he wanders in a world of objects inhabited by man objects. He abandons science, together with subjectivity, steps out of humanity, and substitutes himself for God, whom he denies, to contemplate the spectacle of the universe. Back from his trip, he tells us that everything that is real is rational, which might make sense from a Kantian, but makes none coming from a materialist. If reason is governed from outside, how can it remain reason? Lenin thought it would improve matters to consider consciousness as "the reflection of being, approximately exact in the best cases." But who will determine what the best cases are without idealist criteria or values? In the end, the materialist destroys his metaphysics with his positivism, and his positivism with his rationalism. In fact, by using idealist criteria, he falls back into idealism.[3]

Since a Marxist refuses to debate on a non-Marxist level, Walter Odajnyk, in *Marxism and Existentialism,* tried to formulate the answers which could be offered in defense of the Marxist point of view. When Marxism claims that the mind has its origin in matter, it does not have to postulate some unverifiable spiritual entity in which matter has its origin, and responds physiologically and psychologically; it remains on the plane of science interpreting the world as "various forms of matter interacting with other forms of matter and giving rise to a complex series of phenomena." [4] Materialism is not, therefore, a metaphysical system. To the argument that Marxism assumes the idealist's privilege of contemplating the world from outside to decide on its rationality, the Marxist would reply that his criteria are not the idealist criteria of clarity, distinctness, or permanence, but practice: I know that fire is fire because it burns:

> Reason is an evolutionary product of a mind which attained self-consciousness: a quantitative-qualitative development occurred within man's brain, producing a mind capable of reflecting upon its own actions and upon the laws that guide the world; and therefore even upon the world's development. This is no longer an effect expressing its causes, but an effect contemplating its causes and capable of acting upon those causes. [5]

How the mind can break the chain of causality, Marxism does not care to explain. Causality, to the Marxist, is response to a stimulus, and the response is always the same to the same stimulus. Applied to social conditions, however, the idea of causation is ambiguous: "The recognition of the causal laws which govern society gives man the freedom to act upon these laws and alter them to suit his purposes." [6] At this point, Odajnyk drops his part as spokesman for Marxism, concedes that Sartre is right in finding the freedom in question incompatible with a materialist philosophy, and offers his own criticism of both Marxism and existentialism: "It is the same glaring contradiction in Marxism that keeps coming back again and again: men, ideas, society are determined by operative physical, economic, and social causes, and they can be free of all these causes at times, if not always. Which is it?" [7] Marxism, then, went too far in explaining all behavior through social forces and neglecting individual subjectivity; existentialism fares no better with its subjective yet universally applicable statements.

Odajnyk's version of what a Marxist could say in his defense against Sartre's criticism of Marxist materialism unfolds on the three planes of materialism, positivism, and practicality, each position cancelling the others. To clarify the question, we must go back to Engels' definition of historical materialism. To our surprise, we find that, not as a second thought but from the very start, it is given as nothing else than British sensationalism: "Materialism is the natural-born son of Great Britain. . . . Nominalism, the first form of materialism, is found chiefly among the English schoolmen. . . ." Engels goes on, quoting Marx himself:

". . . the real progenitor of English materialism is Bacon. To him natural philosophy is the only true philosophy, and physics based upon the experience of the senses is the chief part of natural philosophy. . . . According to him, the senses are infallible and the source of all knowledge. All science is based on experience, and consists in subjecting the data furnished by the senses to a rational method of investigation. . . . Among the qualities inherent in matter, motion is the first and foremost, not only in the form of mechanical and mathematical motion, but chiefly in the form of an impulse, a vital spirit, a tension—or a *'qual,'* to use a term of Jakob Böhme's—of matter. . . .

"Hobbes had systematized Bacon without, however, furnishing a proof for Bacon's fundamental principle, the origin of all human knowledge from the world of sensation. It was Locke who, in his *Essay concerning Human Understanding,* supplied the proof." [8]

Locke is the father, not only of "that brilliant school of French materialists which made the eighteenth century . . . a pre-eminently French century," but also, through Condillac, Destutt de Tracy, and Auguste Comte, of positivism as well. It was Comte who definitely gave up metaphysics for positive facts, associated theology with feudalism, tried to raise the scientific method to the level of philosophy, and decided that human behavior could only be studied through the new science of "sociology." As a form of positivism, Marxism is entirely consistent. Why then did Marx insist on calling it "materialism," since, as Sartre rightly claims, materialism is a metaphysical hypothesis concerning the totality of the universe? Furthermore, why did Engels define matter as an impulse, a vital spirit, a tension, and claim the authority of the arch-mystic Jakob Böhme to find in matter a *"qual,"* strictly the pain resulting from that inward tension? This last point might be clarified by the examination of the second area of dissent: the claim of Marxist materialism to be dialectical.

2. THE DIALECTICAL ASPECT OF MARXIST MATERIALISM

Dialectics, Sartre claims, makes sense in an idealistic system where the thesis brings forth the antithesis as being originally part of the same totality, but makes none in a materialistic system. Matter is a sum, not a totality. (Even Einstein's relationships remain quantitative and external.) To make of materialism a philosophy of opposition is nonsense. There is no opposition in matter; whatever opposites we see in it are projections of human subjectivity: hot is not the opposite of cold, it is a higher temperature. Qualitative changes (as Bergson had claimed) characterize the mind, as quantitative changes characterize matter. Briefly then, Sartre refuses to see in matter the dialectical process of affirmation, negation, and negation of the negation, which is perfectly rational in Hegel's objective idealism, but is nothing else, applied to a materialistic universe, than a crude sort of magic.

The Marxist, states Odajnyk, could maintain that dialectics is valid, at least as a method of scientific investigation, applied to matter, life, or society, and would reject Sartre's claim that, according to the very idea of synthesis, life cannot be reduced to matter, nor human consciousness to life. He would reject Sartre's assertion that matter is inertia, evolution a process of progressive elimination, and dialectics a system that can work only with ideas. As reflections, ideas reflect the objective world. It is not true that only quantitative changes can take place in matter. The changes from water to ice, from the acorn to the tree, are qualitative and dialectical changes, and so are all the changes taking place generally in evolution. We realize that the term "dialectics" itself may have gone through some similar transformation, and Odajnyk admits that its meaning had to be stretched considerably to fit into a materialistic doctrine. He seems to prefer this form of excess to a view of nature which reduces evolution to the principle of inertia, and nature to absolute anarchy and chaos.

Before trying to reach a conclusion on this debate, let us find out what definition of the term "dialectics" was offered by the founders of Marxism. This definition can be found in Engels' book against Dühring, first published in 1880. Dialectics is given in this work as the contribution of German philosophy to the Anglo-French, scientifically-oriented "materialism" which we have identified with positivism, and to the Franco-British utopian socialism of St. Simon, Fourier, and Owen. To St. Simon, indeed, Marxism owes the rewriting of history according to the evolution of the means of production; and Engels admits that in St. Simon's works is found, already very clearly expressed, "the idea of the future conversion of political rule into an administration of things and a direction of processes of production." [9] (Engels fails to mention the fact that such a direction was to be entrusted to a natural aristocracy based on "capacities.") He praises Fourier for his criticism of the universal duplicity which forms the basis of modern society, but ignores his clumsy efforts to formulate a social organization based on harmony, wherein liberated passions would play the same part as universal attraction in the Newtonian system. He seems to admire without restriction Fourier's history of humanity, and its division into the four stages of savagery, barbarism, the patriarchate, and civilization; but fails to mention that Fourier had predicted for the future a period of *garantisme* (welfare state) to be followed by the triumph of "association." Finally, Engels shows at length that it was Robert Owen who first established, through practical experiment as well as in theory, the theory of accumulation of capital through appropriation of surplus value, which was to form the basis of Marx's *Capital*.

Utopian socialism, then, had formulated the main economic theories of Marxism; yet it had failed in three revolutions or had died in isolated experiments. That, claims Engels, was because its founders thought that it is "the expression of absolute truth, reason, and justice, and has only to be discovered to conquer all the world by virtue of its own power." [10] To become operative, socialism had to insert itself into history, and to become dialectical. Dialectics was to be the contribution of Hegel's philosophy, "placed on its feet," i.e., on a materialistic basis, to Franco-British socialism.

Engels then explains what he and Marx understand by dialectics. From the first, we discover that the Marxist definition of dialectics is far more comprehensive than Hegel's. The early Greek philosophers, Aristotle, Descartes, Spinoza, and Rousseau were all dialecticians in their own way. The source of dialectics is given as Heraclitus:

> When we consider and reflect upon nature at large or the history of mankind or our own intellectual activity, at first we see the picture of an endless entanglement of relations and reactions, permutations and combinations, in which nothing remains what, where, and as it was, but everything moves, changes, comes into being, and passes away. We see, therefore, at first the picture as a whole, with its individual parts still more or less kept in the background; we observe the movements, transitions, connections rather than the things that move, combine, and are connected. This primitive, naïve, but intrinsically correct conception of the world is that of ancient Greek philosophy, and was first clearly formulated by Heraclitus: everything is and is not, for everything is fluid, is constantly changing, constantly coming into being and passing away.[11]

To understand the details of this general picture, scientists, throughout the ages, had to detach them from their natural and historical surroundings and this method of work has left us as legacy "the habit of observing natural objects and processes in isolation, apart from their connection, with the vast whole; of observing them in repose, not in motion, as constants, not as essentially variables; in their death, not in their life." [12] This strangely Bergsonian pronouncement shows that a certain amount of vitalism has crept into Marxist positivism, or was there from the first, as a legacy of German romanticism. Bacon and Locke, in fact, are now accused by Engels of transferring from science to philosophy a narrow and static way of thought.

Sartre's claim that dialectical materialism is absurd because there can be no opposition in matter, is no longer valid, if we remember that Marx considered motion, among the qualities inherent in matter, "not only in the form of mechanical and mathematical motion, but chiefly in the form of a vital spirit—or a *"qual,"* to use a term of Jakob Böhme's—matter. . . ." It seems strange that Marx should seek the explanation of motion in Böhme, who may be the source of Newton's theory of universal attraction, but is also surely the main source of Hegel's absolute idealism. Newton's appeal to the utopian socialists was that he gratified their romantic yearning to endow matter with the attributes of the spirit. Modern physics seems to confirm the possibility of a dialectical process in matter, but it is a dialectics of being and non-being, non-being in this case figuring as a void which, strangely enough, can react like the Sartrean *Néant.* This void is the negation of being and it is also, at the same time, being itself.[13] If modern science, then, confirms the possibility of dialectics in matter, it is a dialectics of being and non-being which Sartre might accept, in fact, vaguely suggests in his hypothesis that motion might be a lesser being, and a first attempt of the in-itself to become its own foundation. If dialectics exists in matter for modern science, it is at the expense of the traditional concept of "matter." Neither the scientists who speculate on the theory of "anti-matter," nor the Jesuit Teilhard de Chardin can strictly be called materialists. Problems dealing with the mystery of matter and of life will rest, in the last analysis, with the philosophically-minded scientists rather than with the scientifically-minded philosophers or sociologists.

3. SOCIAL DIALECTICS IN MARXISM

As applied to society, materialist dialectics claims that past history is the history of class struggles and that the classes of society are the products of the modes of production and exchange:

> . . . in a word, of the *economic* conditions of their time; that the economic structure of society always furnishes the real basis, starting from which we can alone work out the ultimate explanation of the whole superstructure of juridical and political institutions, as well as of the religious, philosophical, and other ideas of a given historical period.[14]

In our age, individual means of production have changed into *social* means of production workable only by a collectivity of men, while appropriation of its surplus value has remained individual. This contradiction contains the germ of the social antagonisms between the bourgeoisie and the proletariat.

According to Marxist dialectics, consciousness then is only the reflection of a given situation. The conditions of material life in society, says Stalin, determine its ideas, its theories, and its political opinions; but he also states that "new ideas are brought by new tasks to be accomplished." How can we, says Sartre, believe both affirmations? Is the idea determined by the social conditions, or is it brought about, or suggested by new tasks to be accomplished? The last statement implies finality. This would seem to dispose of the so-called materialist dialectics as applied to society.

Identification of a given philosophy with a moment of class culture is nevertheless, as Odajnyk observes, Marxism's favorite and most damaging form of criticism. To the Marxist, existentialism is the expression of a moment of dying bourgeois culture. Marxism has no difficulty in finding the roots of existentialism in Christianity and connecting the whole picture of man's estrangement in modern society to the forlorn position of the individual in the capitalist world. Sartre himself recognized that it was Marx who first pointed out that in capitalist society man becomes a thing among things and that relationships among people are determined by those things. Odajnyk makes the interesting observation that Marxism and existentialism detect in each other a religious element and a bourgeois origin. He suggests that possibly Marxism may have influenced existentialism in some of its better traits.[15] Let us note, however, that while existentialism tends to secularize religious symbols, themes, and feelings, Marxism, by contrast, turns into religious dogma the basic tenets of irreligious thinking. As to the bourgeois origin of Marxism, the Marxists would no doubt point out that with Marx it was only a dialectical moment, while Sartrean existentialism remains branded with bourgeois individualism. Both Marxism and Sartrean existentialism seem to take it for granted that the salvation of the working classes can only come from middle-class intellectuals. Marx and Engels manage to reconcile this fact with their all-embracing dialectics, according to which the class in power works out its downfall while clinging desperately to its privileges; Sartrean existentialism would have a harder time explaining how liberty could be conferred from outside, since, in its extreme subjectivism, it claims each consciousness is equally free from any situation and must work out its own salvation from that situation. From this point of view, it would seem that American trade unionism, or French syndicalism, should constitute the ideal pattern of liberation. Yet, this is not the case. Sartre's ideal appears to consist in some sort of cooperation between the *petit bourgeois intellectuel* and the working class.

The theory concerning "superstructures," the most original and the most startling contribution of Marxism, would nevertheless, if taken literally, place the Marxist in the situation of the Cretan who claimed that all Cretans were liars. If any philosophy, at any given moment, is no more than the expression of a given economic system, interpreted by a certain social class, it has no more validity than any other system. Materialism may be the fitting philosophy of the proletariat, in the same way as dualism was, in the baroque age, the philosophy of the higher-middle-class, and as idealism has always been, from Plato onward, the philosophy of the aristocracy. Histories of literature absentmindedly record that fact when they contrast the "courtly literature" of the Middle Ages with the "bourgeois literature" which slowly took its place, a similar evolution taking place in theology, from Plato to Aristotle, during the same period. But each class may have its glimpse of the total truth, and the values discarded by one age have a way of persisting underground to reassert themselves in another.

Marxism is right, then, to call our attention to the fact that what we take to be a philosophy of life is often the expression of class culture; it contradicts itself when it asserts itself as the only valid philosophy. Its claim to derive class culture exclusively from economic conditions seems also excessive. Feudalism, no doubt, was connected with an economic system, but it is difficult to say with absolute certainty which was the product of the other. The rise of an aristocracy which placed courage above all values is better explained by Hegel's theory of the master-to-slave relation, bearing as it does on an age of universal conflict when one had to choose between bondage and contempt for one's life. *Noblesse oblige* survived the feudal age, and a curious acknowledgment of its persistence as value may be found in the pride taken by Marx himself in his marriage with a girl from the nobility. A similar reverence for a supposedly dead ideal makes Mathieu, in *L'Age de raison,* drive a knife through his hand, in emulation of Ivich, to prove that a French *petit bourgeois intellectuel* could rise up to the level of a young girl from the Russian nobility. Marxism does not hesitate, any more than existentialism, to demand from its followers an extreme heroism which may fit in with a philosophy of liberty but hardly with a materialistic system. Again we must consult Marx and Engels for an explanation of this paradox.

4. LIBERTY AND MATERIALISM; THE CONVENIENT MYTH

Most of the inconsistencies denounced by Sartre in Marxism stem from its proclaimed materialism. Materialism is in every way unexpected from a social creed aiming at helping the majority of mankind to find a freer and fuller life. Yet freedom is given as the true aim of Marxism:

> Freedom . . . consists in the control over ourselves and over external nature which is founded on knowledge of natural necessity; it is therefore a product of historical development. The first men who separated themselves from the animal kingdom were in all essentials as unfree as the animals themselves, but each step forward in civilization was a step toward freedom.[16]

To obtain freedom, the first condition required is the appreciation of necessity. "Freedom of the will therefore means nothing but the capacity to make decisions with real knowledge of the subject. Therefore the *freer* a man's judgment is in relation to a definite question, with so much the greater necessity is the content of this judgment determined. . . ." [17]

We can see now how far removed from materialistic determinism original Marxism was in the mind of its founders. Neither through its conception of matter, nor in its theory of social evolution, does Marxism concede that human behavior is actually determined by external necessity:

> No. Men make their history themselves, only they do so in a given environment, which conditions it, and on the basis of actual relations already existing, among which the economic relations, however much they may be influenced by the other, the political and ideological relations, are still ultimately the decisive ones, forming the keynote which runs through them and alone leads to understanding.[18]

Truly, Marxism does admit, as most modern sociologists do, that individual consciousness is, to begin with, conditioned by a given social consciousness, and even more so, by class consciousness; but this conditioning is not given as a determining factor, since members of the ruling class are regularly expected to help the underprivileged class to rise to power.

As one reads Marx and Engels, one must admit in all honesty, that such reading is a pleasant relief from the sonorous platitudes of today's Marxism. To begin with, they make excellent reading, even in translation. Their main weapon is the unrelenting irony which is characteristic of that other rebellious son of Hegel, Kierkegaard. One can only respect them for their generous indignation at the unimaginable conditions prevailing in the industrial world of their times. They never try to force their system on any given historical situation, but take great pains to account for all its intricacies, or complexity. Neither do they eliminate from their interpretation of history factors which do not fit with their main thesis, such as the peculiarities of the national British, French, or German character. Even in social theory, they are broad-minded enough to admit that "the bourgeoisie during its rule of scarce one hundred years, has created more massive and colossal productive forces than have all preceding generations together." [19] Engels' praise of colonial rule in Algeria, unprintable in the Marxist press, would have scandalized liberal opinion during the recent years of conflict. Their program, as formulated in the Communist Manifesto, included, among ten items, some of which would still be considered subversive in democratic countries, many reforms which have been accepted or are thought desirable in these countries, both in Europe and in America, such as: the progressive tax, the centralization of credit in the hands of the state, gradual abolition of the distinction between town and country, the cultivation of waste lands, free education for all children in public schools, and abolition of children's factory labor.

Shall we conclude, like Sartre, that authentic Marxism is dead? Shall we absolve Marxism of all the crimes committed in its name? Unfortunately, one can never become completely convinced that any belief, faith, or ideology is to be completely exonerated of the crimes and follies that follow in its trail. Closer analysis of the doctrine generally reveals some hidden defect responsible for its deviation. In this particular instance, we feel that Sartre was right in denouncing in Marxism the materialism which, apparently to conform with the situation of the oppressed class, turned men into men-objects for the convenience of the future dictators of the masses.

We may grant that materialism is the most natural philosophy for men who have been alienated from the product of their labor, the philosophy that will reach their heart and soul, instill into them the feeling of their objectification and, through a natural dialectical process, force them to assume and negate simultaneously that objectivity. The only result of that process, however, will be to make them want to objectivate their masters in turn, as Spartacus' gladiators made sport of forcing Roman citizens to fight each other to death, just to affirm their own freedom.

Granting that, unlike Spartacus, the Marxists had a program carefully thought out when they took over—as they generally do—a revolution fought out by others, their main purpose in enforcing their "materialist" doctrine could only be to perpetuate the slave mentality which they, as rulers, found most convenient to create some continuity between the rule of the exploiters and their own. Materialism in this case was not accepted without some mental restriction as far as they were concerned; it was materialism for others. Such bad faith is easier to fall into than one thinks. Prohibition would not have been so easily accepted if each one had not thought it a good thing for others. Religion is often encouraged for a similar reason. In last analysis, every one counting on the other to accept the convenient myth, the moment arrives when every one in turn becomes tired of playing the part of "the other." Materialism, closely considered, is such a myth; it is always materialism for others.

The Marxists will retort that, whether their philosophy is sound or not, it has been successful; but, concludes Sartre, it has been successful only with the party in power, which has become the sole proprietor of the state.

5. SARTREAN MARXISM

If there is one point on which most critics seem to be in agreement concerning Sartre's *Critique de la raison dialectique,* it is that this work is cumbersome, repetitious, and unnecessarily difficult. Some of the readers who plunge into it, with the conviction that nothing Sartre writes could be a matter of total indifference, have to give up before the end. The academic mind will shrink from it, in the same way as Cardinal Bembo shrank from the Old Testament in fear of spoiling his style, and for the same reason. The style of the *Critique* has a ponderous monotony, and its deadly seriousness suggests the possibility that, if man is still totally free starting from a given situation, the grip of necessity severely restricts his liberties to certain narrow paths. Wilfrid Desan's *The Marxism of Jean-Paul Sartre* offers the layman a clarified yet minutely complete presentation of Sartre's attempted fusion of existentialism and Marxism. Chapter VII of Odajnyk's *Marxism and Existentialism* presents a condensed, yet very thorough, analysis, based on the latter work, followed by an interesting account of the fortunes of Sartre's effort in Marxist countries. My purpose here is, as stated above, to establish some logical connections between Sartrean Marxism and the philosophy of *L'Etre et le Néant* so as to clarify, as far as it is possible, the evolution of Sartre's thought.

Sartre admits that the fascination of Marxism, to him and other *petits bourgeois intellectuels* of his generation, was, from the start, its practical character, the fact that it was *lived* and *practiced,* on his horizon, by "the enormous and somber body" of working masses.[20] The real difficulty for him was to pass from the plane of mere comprehension to the plane of *praxis,* i.e., thought related to action. While, on the philosophical plane, materialism seemed completely unacceptable to him, he now accepts it, as limited by Marx's formula: "The mode of production of material life in general dominates the development of social, political, and intellectual life." [21] This is just a practical consideration, and "materialism" thus understood now appears to Sartre compatible with a certain kind of dialectics more akin, as we shall see, to existentialism than to Marxism.

Marxism, to him, is the only valid interpretation of history; but existentialism is the only concrete approach to reality, because it starts and stays with the actual situation of individual consciousness in the Here and Now. To Marxism, the truth of the individual is in society, while, to Sartre, the truth of society is in the individual. It is then a question for him to raise the study of the structures of consciousness to the level of sociology and history, without ever yielding to the temptation of considering the group, the class, or the nation as an organic entity. The enterprise is arduous, for if it is true that society is made up of individuals and is in itself no more than an abstraction, this abstraction is a most convenient one for the study of collectivities, since integrated collectivities behave as if they were organic bodies, with a life and a unity of their own. Transferring his philosophy from the level of individual behavior to the level of collective behavior, Sartre finds it necessary to adapt his vocabulary to this new plane.

To begin with, we find that the void, or "lack" of the for-itself, or consciousness, with its constant yearning for the concreteness of the in-itself, or being, is replaced by the notion of *need,* or *scarcity.* Scarcity is the dominant feature of our present world; scarcity of food, scarcity of living space, and scarcity of goods are the basis of the natural conflict between conscious-

nesses, prior to the need for recognition illustrated in *No Exit*.
Man is haunted by the possibility of being deprived of what he
needs through the existence of the other. This basic conflict need
not take the form of war; it may take the form of a voluntary
limitation of the population and is present in the Marxist as well
as in the democratic world, as testified—I may add—by the
present hostility between Russia and China. Man is responsible
for that scarcity upon which he has conferred value in building
up his history. Through man, scarcity has become an attribute
of matter—as we see in the value attached to gold—and, through
a sort of dialectical process, scarcity reaches man through matter.
If there is a dialectics of nature, therefore, it is only insofar as
human *praxis* confers upon matter its specific value. One can
see how Sartre manages to reconcile his former viewpoint, according to which there can be no dialectics in matter, with his
desire to come closer to the practical aspect of Marxist materialism.

It is, then, in the course of the practical activity exercised
to gratify his needs, that the individual takes a total view of
his surroundings and *totalizes* them. The result of that totalization is a *totality* which, we must remember, is not to be considered as an original situation encountered by consciousness,
but as projected by man on the diversity of things in the light of
his *praxis*. No longer is individual consciousness, as consciousness, the center of reference of a totalitarian organization of the
world; in other words, no longer does consciousness, as absolute
negation and pure non-being, project to acquire through the
world the concreteness of being, which it lacks. We are dealing
primarily with basic, physical needs.

The totality in question is not active, like Hegel's Totality
of Mind; it is a passive sort of totality which opposes its inertia
to man's *praxis*. For that reason, Sartre calls it a *practico-inert*
totality. As such, however, and whether it is made up of things
or of other people, considered more or less as objects, it tends to

limit and to mold the free consciousness which contends with it.

As an obstacle to freedom, this practico-inert totality constitutes the "anti-dialectic." Obviously, through this term, Sartre intends to reserve the term "dialectic" to the free activity of consciousness, in accordance with his former philosophy and with his criticism of materialistic dialectics. Nevertheless, this notion of inertia reacting upon a free activity, so that everything happens as if there had been actually a sort of exchange between mind and matter, is so disconcerting in Sartre's new terminology that I cannot refrain from referring the reader to the Bergsonian interpretation of similar exchanges taking place in human intelligence between the attributes of mind and the attributes of matter, between those of the organic and those of the inorganic. If the unity of mind and freedom is projected on the multiplicity of things, outside of consciousness, the mind, conversely, becomes imbued with the attributes of matter, quantity and externality, through which it has tried to liberate itself. In other words, the mind, having projected its unity into things, reflects in turn upon itself their multiplicity, externality, objectivity, in short their materiality.

6. DIALECTICS IN SARTREAN MARXISM

With these data in mind, we are now ready to study, from the viewpoint of the individual consciousness, the formation of collectivities. In *No Exit,* we had three consciousnesses freed, for the excellent reason that they are in Hell, from the *practical* problems of existence. The reason why there were three of them is that a group of three persons is to Sartre a convenient and simplified representation of society. In the *Critique,* the three persons representing the social drama in its most elementary form are not in Hell. One of them is looking through the window of his house (thanks to his living there, a "practico-inert totality") at two workmen absorbed by two different tasks, who do not see each other. Fully aware that they are two individual workmen, intent on the realization of two distinct practical projects, the *third man* identifies them as belonging to the same category of persons, and confers upon them the unity of their class as workmen. Extending his illustration, Sartre imagines a taxi driver driving along the Seine and catching sight of a group of people watching something going on in the river. Absorbed by whatever is going on, these people are not conscious of constituting a group but, to the taxi driver, conscious of the fact that a common interest keeps them together, they are a group. The group unity is conferred upon them from outside by the taxi driver. Or else, Sartre imagines a group of people waiting for the autobus, each one anxiously looking for the appearance of the vehicle which is to take them to the various tasks they want to perform. In this case, it is a material object, the autobus, which, as a common objective, creates the unity of the group.

In the same way, men living within definite areas, and trying to overcome scarcity, are unified by common needs; and the trespassing of their common ground may cause wars. Scarcity is what binds the group together; and, as we saw, scarcity is projected into matter by man himself. As far as the individual is concerned, he is still free within the group, free, we take it, to leave the group, with whatever consequences to himself.

To these preliminary considerations, we must add the fact that there is a certain *alienation* which comes to man from the very products of his work. He recognizes himself in his work; yet he has also become foreign to it. In *L'Etre et le Néant,* Sartre granted man a sort of symbolic gratification in the creation of objects which were like an extension of the for-itself, yet with an in-itself life of their own. There is no question of such gratification now; rather the object is like an objectification of the self. It is a commonplace statement in our age that the machine is a man-made monster which might end by getting out of control and fashion men's life in its turn. Absolute standardization and a general uniformity are often considered to be the unavoidable results of the reign of the machine, and the penalty paid for the gratification of the needs of the greatest number. The relative optimism of such statements reveals a certain human complicity in the triumph of the machine. Its dire consequences: air pollution, an inhuman scenery, the monotony of factory work, etc., are from the start, according to Sartre, tacitly accepted by the employer and the employee. In this dialectics of man *vs.* the machine, man remains free and responsible. He accepts the dictates of his own invention; its consequences are not his primary intention, but they cannot be dissociated from his intention. The reign of the machine prepares that of the anonymous and inexistent human being who was identified with Heidegger's *das man* in *L'Etre et le Néant,* and who now bears the name of "the other." The machine dictates the way in which it should be handled, creating the habits of mind which Sartre formerly defined as the "spirit of seriousness." Not only the consumers but the producers as well become, through publicity and competition, the willing victims of this situation; for publicity must pressure the prospective buyer into the way of life a hypothetical "other" has already adopted, while competition is at once dependence on the other and negation of the other. By placing his *interest* in the machine, the employer has his being outside of himself. He becomes the representative of the machine, while the worker becomes part of the practico-inert world as its manipulator.

The originality of Sartre in these observations is not in the facts revealed, but in his desperate endeavor to interpret them, at each step of his argument, in harmony with his theory of liberty. Things only reflect the totalization that man has projected into things.

7. SOCIAL DIALECTICS

As part of the "practico-inert" world, man discovers himself in a collective body made up of a juxtaposition of individuals: the *series*. By the term "series," Sartre designates the non-integrated crowd of people who happen to find themselves together without any decision on their part: fellow-travellers, fellow-citizens, fellow-workers. There is of course a reason why they are together but they have not chosen to be. To each other, they are just *other* individuals, and otherness is the only character they have in common. A series is an inorganic social entity. Each one in the series feels that he is just another person, and feels the solitude of his otherness.

How an inorganic and amorphous conglomeration of individuals can be turned into an organic, integrated group has been humorously described by the writer Jules Romains in a number of plays and novels. What is remarkable in all of the cases is the casual way in which the integration takes place, and the fragility of the bond which brings the individuals together into a group with a collective soul. It may be the doing of some adventurer, the presence of a socialist inscription on a wall, the death of an unknown worker in an apartment house. It seems as if the non-integrated collectivity was waiting for the slightest pretext to acquire its soul. This is precisely what Romains wants to prove. Society, according to Romains' unanimism, is not a sum but a totality, a *psychic continuum*. This does not mean that the collectivity is always ready to become integrated, on any ideological level. In Romains' best known play, *Knock,* a modern quack in search of a clientele takes care to find out exactly whether the inhabitants of the little town where he plans to practice are free of spiritual, political, commercial, or sexual obsessions or passions, before he decides that they are ripe for the "medical age." The rest is a matter of psychology and organization: a doctoral thesis as a sacred text, publicity, education, and appeal to the various social classes.

Sartre completely rejects the theory of a mysterious Totality of Mind presiding over human collectivities. Yet his own conclusions on that question are rather ambiguous. From a metaphysical viewpoint, Hegel is right: "it is the point of view of the totality which is the right point of view, the true point of view":

> Everything happens as if the others and myself were marking the vain effort of a totality of being-for-itself to get hold of itself again and encompass what it *has to be* on the pure and simple mode of the in-itself.[22]

Yet, being-for-others can exist only through a separateness which no totality, even the totality of Mind, can produce. Sartre is no closer to Hegel today than when he made the preceding statement in *L'Etre et le Néant*. Neither is he closer to Marx than to Hegel on this point. His aim is to show how a sum of individuals can become an organized body, or, to use his terminology, how a series can become a *group,* through the consciousness of each individual in the series.

As we learned from *L'Etre et le Néant,* it is only through the realization of common objectification, and negation of that objectification, that a collectivity can pass from the "us-object" to the "we-subject," in common *praxis,* or action. During this dynamic process, the group is what Sartre calls *le groupe en fusion.* The example chosen by Sartre is the storming of the Bastille in 1789. The section of Paris which surrounds the Bastille feels threatened by the cannons of the fortress as well as by the army rumored to be outside of the city. It feels objectified inasmuch as each citizen has been turned into a psychical object, a transcended-transcendence, as part of the crowd; in other words, he is like a fugitive from justice whose every move is foreseen, in time as in space. This situation is already familiar to us through the description of *L'Etre et le Néant;* in this case, however, the citizen of the district does not feel threatened as a common, isolated, criminal. He is threatened as a member of the district, known for its turbulence.

For the citizens to pass from the consciousness of a common objectification to the assertion of a common subjectivity, it is essential that each citizen should first of all affirm his own subjectivity as an individual consciousness, yet, at the same time, that each citizen should fuse with the group, for common action to be possible. How can this phenomenon take place?

A romantic historian, Michelet, was struck by the spontaneous character of the movement which led to the storming of the Bastille. There cannot be any such group spontaneity for Sartre. Sartre does not believe in any psychic continuum, unanimism, or Totality of Mind, underlying the multiplicity of minds, to help the group find its collective soul. The process of collective fusion must be explained through the individual reaction of each individual consciousness.

Each individual consciousness feels threatened and objectified as part of a crowd; yet, at the same time, it is liberated from this objectification by the fact that the whole district is also threatened. He stands, in relation to the threatened district and the forces that threaten the district, in the position of the third man, such as we saw it, dialectically depicted, in *No Exit*. In this play, each consciousness in turn was free to view the conflict between the other two, as an outsider, and thereby to objectify the object-to-subject relation between them. In the *Critique*, it was the man at the window who, as a spectator, conferred upon the two workers the unity of a practico-inert totality: "The third man emerges both as human *organizer* of a unity and as human part of the unity." [23]

This convergence of supposedly incompatible subjectivities is, of course, a rare phenomenon, favored by a moment of high historical tension. The group coalesced in the heat of action; and to Sartre, as we know, it is only in action that human subjectivities, turned toward a common objective, can abolish the original conflict between consciousnesses:

> Thus, through the coexistence of two structures, one of them being the possible and future negation of the other (and at the same time the negation of all in each one), each one continues to see himself in the other but sees himself in the Other as *himself*, i.e. in this case, as the totalization in himself of the Parisian popu-

lation, through the sword thrust or gunshot which will exterminate him.[24]

Imitation (in which the sociologist Tarde saw the main principle of social cohesion) allows each one in such situations to see in the other his own future, and to discover his present act in the act of the other; in other words, the distinction between my act and the other's act tends to vanish in common *praxis*.

Even in this privileged moment, one can detect signs of incipient organization. Any third man can suggest the next move, and it is freely accepted as intended to result in victory, but a certain amount of inertia may develop, leading individuals to accept such suggestions as orders.

The next, and unavoidable, stage in the evolution of the group is the passage from the *groupe en fusion* to the *group under oath*. Since the individuals in the group are no longer bound together by action against a common enemy, they bind themselves together through fear of penalty. This sort of agreement constitutes what Sartre calls the *fraternity-terror* regime. Sartre may be obsessed by the dramatic form assumed by this agreement during the French Revolution, but the "oath," as a means of enforcing social cohesion, is by no means outdated, and the "terror" element may take milder forms than the fear of being driven to the guillotine in a tumbril cart. The fear of being ostracized as not belonging to the group may play the same part in a status-seeking society. To quote Desan:

> In truth, the *terreur* is actually a natural development of a group, any group. It is not a minority dictating its will through violence, but it is myself and all of us involved in a mutual distrust and a mutual hope, the hope of consolidating the group through consolidating the inert within us.[25]

The group then is bound, by its collective character, to turn into an *institution*. In an institution, the individual becomes inessential and the function essential. The common objective remains, but a certain amount of inertia has developed with organization, together with distrust of individual initiative and impotency toward alteration. We cannot help detecting some similarity between the change from the *groupe en fusion* to the *institution,* and the Bergsonian dialectics of the open and closed groups. In both systems, at least, it is individual consciousness which represents dynamism and initiative and the institution which represents the restrictive and conservative element. Sartre, however, manages to explain the passage from individual *praxis* to social *processus.*

The institutionalized group evolves into the State which, to Sartre, means only the domination of a social class, then into a *bureaucracy,* which, in principle, is supposed to convey the wishes of the lower classes through the appropriate channels, to the governing class, but is in fact only a system through which the class in power conditions the lower social levels to "adjustment" through the appropriate institutions. By then *praxis* has become *processus.*

8. CONCLUSION

Just as Marx claimed to have made Hegel stand on his feet, Sartre could claim to have forced Marx to stand both on his feet and on his head. Sartre's dialectics is not, like Engels', of the kind that defines events as the resultant of a parallelogram of forces. Sartrean dialectics is rather in the opposition between freedom and inertia, consciousness and the world. Thus, Desan is justified in calling Sartre the last of the Cartesians. Sartre's main concern is still to save consciousness from the status of otherness and objectivity conferred upon it from outside.

Truly, in Sartre's social philosophy, the feeling of scarcity takes the place of the anguish of non-being, the for-itself becomes the dialectic, the in-itself becomes the anti-dialectic, the us-object becomes the series, the we-subject becomes the group, but the totalitarian organization of the world around the self as center of reference is still brought about by consciousness under the process of totalization. This new vocabulary is the concrete indication of a last stand to defend the *cogito.* Words are the fortresses of thought; they have the merit of consolidating a position, at the risk of constituting an anti-dialectic of their own and killing the spirit. It is not certain, however, that Sartre's new positions mark an advance over those reached in *L'Etre et le Néant.* The notion of scarcity, no matter how valid in the history of primitive civilizations, does not account for all human activities as completely as the all-embracing value of the in-itself-for-itself. Scarcity can hardly be the basis of all conflicts. To prove this, one does not have to situate three consciousnesses in the Hell of *No Exit,* where needs are inexistent; one has only to observe them in a place where all needs are satisfied, the American army for instance, to see them fight for the imaginary distinction of a stripe, the more so as they have known more misery before. The dialectics of freedom and inertia, brought down from Bergsonian imaginative as-if philosophy to the discipline of phenomenology, assumes an almost magical character which does not always make comprehension easy. Thus the dumb obstinacy of things "negates" man (perhaps as a concession to Marxist materialism), but we have to understand that matter has been humanized by man's *praxis.* The same idea was more clearly suggested by Bergson, even if Sartre's analysis is closer to reality, as lived by human consciousness. The study of group dynamics, the kind of micro-sociology which permits us to pass from the series to the group, from the group to the institution, is new and represents a progress from *L'Etre et le Néant,* Romains' unanimism, or Bergson's dialectics of the closed and open groups. It does constitute a critique of dialectical reason, and a healthy reminder of the fact that consciousness is an absolute and that man makes his history. But whether society is, or is not, a living organism, the fact remains that, by reason of its inertia, it can be made the object of a science; and no Marxist, or sociologist, who has managed to get a grasp of its laws will relinquish his techniques for the complicated dialectics of a philosophy of liberty which has to concede that society operates more or less as a whole. Psychoanalysis is supposed to complete Sartre's sociology, and to allow us to realize, through the regressive-progressive method, what is unique about the life and character of a Robespierre, a Napoleon, a Baudelaire, or a Flaubert. I must admit here that this method appears to me as inhuman in its method as it is unsatisfactory in its results. Sartre's study of Baudelaire is a well-known example of failure to explain the genius through the man. In Sartre's own case, the little boy anxious to play the part of the hero awaited by his peers to save the situation does not explain the genial inspiration which dictated to him the dialectics of being and non-being. The beauty of the intellect is that it transcends the man, even when this faculty is awakened in him by the need of some sort of compensation.

Sartre's fight to bring about a fusion of existentialism and Marxism does not seem to have been successful, either with the Marxists or his existentialist disciples.

In the Marxist camp, Sartre's *Critique* brought out an answer from Schaff, chief philosopher of Polish Marxism: *Marx oder Sartre?* To Schaff, Sartrean dialectics is weak dialectics: *"eine schwache Dialektik,"* ill-defined and lacking in clarity. The thesis that men make their own history from given situations does not progress through negations of historical determinism, but through specific interpretation of the mechanism through which their determinism operates.[26] At the root of the misunderstanding is a different conception of dialectics and of liberty. Sartre will have either to give up existentialism if he wants to endorse Marxism, or abandon Marxism if he wants to remain faithful to his existentialism.

In this country's Marxist press, Sartre's attempt received an even worse reception. It is interpreted in *News & Letters,* October 1963, as "Sartre's Search of a Method to Undermine Marxism":

> Before . . . we jump to the conclusion that Sartre's new theory of scarcity reveals more a scarcity of thought than a material scarcity, let's remember that new reality which did not confront Marx: the state-capitalist societies of Russia and China, which he calls socialist. Consciously or unconsciously, it is for these he created the theory of scarcity.[27]

Raya Dunayevskaya, the author of this article, sees no justification for a theory of scarcity in a time of overproduction and automation, is rather scandalized by the cleavage Sartre introduces between the "passive" masses and the "active" elite, views with irony Sartre's analyses of such "pressing realities" as the genesis of *Madame Bovary,* and does not hesitate to see in their author the upholder of decadent bourgeois values.

In the non-Marxist camp, Sartre won, at the most, a *succès d'estime,* which failed to convince anybody. Odajnyk thinks that he has given a more precise definition of "dialectic" but comes closer to Marxist determinism in his conception of the antidialectic. The only free act of the individual is in the formation of the *groupe en fusion,* and even that is triggered from outside. The individual is free to leave the group any time but only to slip back into "seriality." His responsibility is total only in a metaphysical sense. In fact, Sartre has entrapped himself in the Marxist net: ". . . instead of adding a helpful dose of free and creative Existentialism to deterministic and stultifying Marxism . . . he has buried Existentialism in a Marxism of his own making. . . ." The *Critique* "is an illegitimate child which neither the Marxists nor the Existentialists will acknowledge as their own." [28]

Desan, in spite of his professed admiration for its author, thinks that the *Critique* has raised the problem of totality without solving it. Sartre refuses to see man as part of a totality, and insists on the fact that any totalization is done by man; Desan rejects this conception as mere activism, and believes that Sartre is wrong in rejecting any encompassing Totality, both in the form of Cosmos and human *Totum*. Desan detects in Sartre's thought two forms of dualism. One is an increasing tendency toward Manicheism. I cannot but endorse Desan's observation on this point. Already in *Nausea,* matter was nauseous, and life, in itself, repulsive. This Manicheistic tendency made of *L'Etre et le Néant* a sort of hymn to Non-Being. The very term "being" had a pejorative connotation, and only the for-itself could deliver us from the evil of "being." Berdyaev at least tried to resolve pessimism of the same nature on the metaphysical plane; Sartre's humanism will not permit him to do so. In his latest philosophical work, the anti-dialectic takes the place of "being," but manicheistic dualism remains. The other form of dualism detected by Desan in Sartre is the Cartesian dualism which, if I may add, is perhaps not unrelated to his Manicheism. If Sartre is influenced by Hegel, it is because his basic philosophical formation rests, like that of Frenchmen of his generation, on Descartes and Bergson, and he could find in Hegel's dialectics a corrective to Bergson's intuitionism.

The main merit of the *Critique* lies, nevertheless, in its being a last stand to affirm the absolute dignity of human consciousness through the theory of totalization. Yet as Desan claims, this theory constitutes a "problematic unresolved." If man is the source of totalization, is it not because, through logical necessity, man is originally and primarily, not only part of the totality, as Desan suggests, but the Totality itself? This notion, which does the utmost violence to our common sense, is yet the only one which may, at least in a purely metaphysical sense, allow us to resolve apparently irreconcilable oppositions. It would make it possible to reconcile Sartre's Cartesian humanism, which makes an absolute of consciousness with Hegel's view of the Totality, with due concessions to the dialectics of evolution. It is only in the identity of man and the cosmos that totalization and Totality can, in the last analysis, be harmonized. Sartre's dialectics of being and non-being has its place in the formulation and resolution of the paradox involved by this vast synthesis.*

* To Sartre, and to his readers, the term "existentialism" means Sartrean existentialism, and it has the same significance throughout this essay. It should perhaps be recalled that other philosophies of existence do also bear, if only by implication, on the social problem. Gabriel Marcel's "concrete philosophy" does so by treating the existential category of "having" as a degradation of "being." Emmanuel Mounier's "personalism" would admit certain affinities with communism, were it not for the two plagues of *"Russification"* and totalitariansim.

8

Conclusion:
A Farewell

Our attempt to situate existentialism in modern
thought led us to see in this philosophical attitude what Sartre
claimed it was: a form of humanism, but with imperfectly recognized vitalistic and mystical presuppositions.

Trying to relate existentialism to the vitalistic, humanistic,
and mystical traditions, we found that these three traditions
could be traced back to the Neo-Platonic philosophy of emanation, a relationship less paradoxical than it may seem. Specialists
in these matters have for a long time detected affinities between
the latter and Bergson's philosophy of creative evolution; similarly, it is no mystery that, through Augustine, the same source
can be claimed for the Protestant tradition leading to Kierkegaard, and of the French humanist tradition which found its
secularized expression in *la littérature engagée*. As to the western
mystical tradition, Plato is its recognized father, but Neo-Platonism was not foreign to its evolution into nature mysticism.

Should we try indeed to state what existentialism owes to
each of these three disciplines, we should find a certain amount of
overlapping. The intuitive method is shared by all three in differing degrees, and so too, with differing interpretations, the
feeling that liberty is an absolute value. The world conceived as

a complex of tools, and the sense of total responsibility for one-self and for the whole world become fully comprehensible only within the total framework of the philosophy of evolution. Simi-larly, the ontological reduction, the conception of mind as de-totalized totality, and of knowledge as identity denied, are more clearly understood from the viewpoint of nature mysticism, al-though they are, or because they are, denials of mystical postu-lates.

All forms of existentialism assume a humanistic position insofar as they start from the situation of the thinking self in the Here and Now, while mysticism starts from the conception of Absolute Being, and vitalism tries to retrace Life's progress towards liberty, from the lowest biological forms to the human level. Only in Sartre, however, do we find an attempt to formu-late a pure existentialism unrelated to some form of metaphysi-cal hypothesis. While the attempt is not, in our opinion, entirely successful, one cannot deny that by concentrating on the struc-tures of consciousness immediately accessible to the existent, Sartre has attained a clarity and rigor of demonstration absent from most philosophies of existence. Yet, it is because he refuses to start with epistemology and tries to reduce knowing to being —a semi-mystical approach—that his "phenomenological on-tology" brings us closer to the understanding of our human situ-ation. Between the opacity of things, which he treats as unknow-able contingencies, and the hypothetical pure Being of meta-physics, which he denies or ignores, he has built an amazing structure within which we seem to find our way. This he has done with genial simplicity by using the dimension of non-being as the expression of multiplicity as well as the ground of liberty. In quasi-trinitarian terms, as Stallknecht suggests, but within a collapsed sort of Trinity, consciousness as Spirit assumes the part of the Son, Word, or Logos, becomes its own "intelligible heaven," and is turned into an absolute. To interpret Sartre in terms of the Trinity is not a forced or arbitrary way of trying to understand him; in spite of oneself, one is led by Sartre's metaphors to seek in his philosophy the inverted or truncated structure of Christian dogma.

To our sense of intellectual ease, however, the Sartrean structure feels like a well planned apartment, cut off from its ground and roofless. Its humanistic plane is isolated from the rest of the living world and no values are written on its empty sky; our relation with the world is one of negation and we make our own values. This is no doubt, practically, a true image of our human situation, since we recognize it in Sartre's descriptions. Yet we retain a lingering suspicion that it is not absolutely and completely true. Even on the plane of practical, concrete behavior, we wonder whether we can dismiss all reference to values which we do not make. Sartre's remarkable analysis of love, for instance, as the project to get recognition as both object and subject from another consciousness entails the possibility of love arising between any two consciousnesses, irrespective of elective affinities and aesthetic values. To our common sense, Sartre's analysis appears true but somehow incomplete. Sartre, no doubt, would specify that a human being symbolizes the world background on which he appears and that we aim at the whole world through one human being; even then something would seem to be missing from the picture. Albertine may have symbolized to young Proust her surroundings of seashore and playing young girls, but we cannot dismiss altogether from our imagination the aesthetic value of her appearance to him. The mere grounding of being in consciousness may be the essential part of artistic values, but it does not necessarily produce aesthetic values.

For Sartre, as we know, to ground being in consciousness is the fundamental, although ideal, human value. As such we might make it the basis of an ethical system consisting in assuming our total situation in the light of a liberty which would entail recognition of the other's liberty. Liberty then would become the only value, but that value would remain merely ethical and we need other values, the sense of beauty and the sense of truth, to guide our liberty. No doubt the sense of beauty and the sense of truth are relative to our situation in time and space but, as Baudelaire clearly saw, they separately point to an absolute in which they merge; and while this absolute is ideal and inaccessible, it is through it that relative values separately subsist.

Sartre's commitment was of such a nature as to make him reject any value outside of the humanistic and ethical plane of thought. While he did promise to formulate his ethics some day, he made no such promise in regard to his metaphysics, which remains inconclusive and imperfectly related to his "ontology." We feel somehow that the most complete commitment a philosopher can make is to formulate his metaphysical outlook, for he thereby assumes, according to his means as a philosopher, the totality of the human situation; further, we feel that an ethical system should rest on this commitment, and that lack of it may have something to do with Sartre's delay in formulating his ethics. Sartre himself is fond of quoting from Dostoïevsky the statement that "if God does not exist everything is permitted," precisely to suggest that ethics remains related to some kind of metaphysics, no matter how crude. Remaining in metaphysics on the plane of doubt or negation, he gave, in *L'Existentialisme est un humanisme,* the impression that postulatory atheism was in fact his basic metaphysical principle. Of course it is not so; mere persistence in a negative dialectical moment could not satisfy a philosopher of his stature. Nevertheless it must be admitted that Sartre tends to dwell on negativity in his studies of human behavior. His interpretation of Baudelaire's genius as a sort of adolescent protest against authority, a protest needing authority in order to affirm itself, is a well-known example of this tendency. There is a feeling among recent critics of Sartre that, applying dialectics to his own thought, he no longer feels committed to the philosophy expressed in *L'Etre et le Néant.* Whether or not one can call indifference to one's former works a dialectical process, a committed philosopher can evolve but cannot afford the luxury of simply having "periods" like a modern painter. We would prefer to think that, having been led by the rigor of his demonstration to establish man's total responsibility for himself, others, and the world, from a given situation, he now feels inclined to grant a little less to liberty and much more to the situation. Liberty from a situation is indeed, to that extent, a conditioned liberty; knowing only slavery, the slave can only prove his liberty to himself by rejecting his slavery, were it but to enslave others. Sartre's work is still unfinished, and we cannot tell with certainty what his definitive message will be. Meanwhile, his present effort to make of existentialism a mere ideology derivative of Marxism will be all the more unconvincing to his disciples as he himself brought to their attention the basic inconsistencies of the Marxist doctrine. Should a revision of this doctrine, intended to make it philosophically acceptable, have become Sartre's final commitment, those whose conception of life he has clarified may refuse to follow him in this commitment, as no doubt the neo-Marxists will do, as many of Pascal's greatest admirers have for centuries rejected Pascal's "wager." They will do so the more easily as Sartre's gift of describing regions of consciousness to which one generally does not have access seems to have left him, as his thought became more dogmatic, in the *Critique de la raison dialectique*.

Indeed the dogmatism of his *Critique* reminded some of Sartre's enthusiasts that from the start they had sometimes experienced a certain uneasiness before his excessive trust in "words" as the fortresses of thought. My own doubts as to Sartre's use of certain terms I made bold to express in a work intended to divulge rather than criticize as well as in the course of the present essays. While Sartre himself recently confessed in *Les Mots* awareness of the tendency we have been alluding to, it is doubtful that his disciples will follow him in his present evolution.

According to his own declarations, Sartre is not interested in what those who will follow him will do with his philosophy, convinced as he is that they will necessarily turn it against him.[1] This is perhaps true but not in the way Sartre means it. His disciples might turn against him to remain faithful to what they have learnt from him. As one of them tells us: "we may in the end have been better pupils than he has been a teacher."[2] Rather than seeing existentialism narrowed down to a mere ideology, we would rather see it evolve into a wider philosophical synthesis, with deeper roots in the study of Life, and more daring suggestions as to its metaphysical implications. Sartre would probably tell us that such a synthesis is out of question, inasmuch as the study of Life, existentialism, and metaphysics involves different forms of knowledge and therefore different methods of investigation. Yet it is not the least of his merits to have managed to incorporate into his own ontology elements borrowed from fifteen centuries of philosophy, which elements, if our conclusions are right, were the results of ways of thought and methods entirely different from his own. Hoping to see his own contribution play the part it deserves in the perennial quest for Truth, we can now say farewell to Sartre.

I. EXISTENTIALIST PHILOSOPHY AND EXISTENTIAL ART

Sooner or later, some connection had to be established between the persistent interest in existentialism and the challenge of today's art. These movements being representative of our mid-century, some thinkers were bound to infer that they constitute parallel reactions to the same world situation. This connection would be all the more logical as the concept of situation is a basic element of existentialism.

It should be recalled, however, that, as philosophy, existentialism is concerned with relating, no matter how indirectly, the concept of situation with the quest of an absolute which may be, according to the case, God, Transcendence, Absolute Being, or Absolute Non-Being. The paradox of existentialism is that this quest is carried out from the plane of the Here and Now, i.e., from the situation of the thinking self in the universe, whether the situation consciously assumed is a personal situation, a historical situation, or the situation common to all which goes under the name of human condition. It is part of the human condition to involve a historical and a personal situation, and *vice versa*. This character of universality allows existentialism to function as a philosophy.

A philosophy which starts with the realization of the total situation of the thinking self in the Here and Now cannot proceed with clear and distinct ideas like Descartes'. That situation can only be experienced at first, with great tension and concern, through the revealing moods which by now have become familiar under the names of contingency, absurdity, anguish, responsibility, guilt, and self-alienation.

The function of the philosopher is to rise above the tension of this realization to the plane of the absolute, or, on the contrary, to retain that tension and interpret existential moods in the light of some absolute, which is precisely what makes him an existentialist philosopher.

Such moods are not unknown to the average man; but, if he happens to experience them, his main concern is to take refuge in useful tasks, play activity, or reassuring ways of thought. Doing so, he may still experience the floating anguish which the existentialist calls the sense of self-alienation. The writer, or the artist, may help the layman in his endeavors by providing him with escape literature, escape art, or ideal values, but may also consider it his task consciously to assume his situation in the Here and Now to make others conscious of that situation. Further than that, the writer or the artist need not go, since he does not have to interpret his description in terms of some absolute. In this respect, the writer may be closer to the philosopher than is the artist, but I think it a mistake to consider the works of Kafka, Malraux, Saint Exupéry, or even Camus, as existentialist literature. The artist is even less of an existentialist since the field of abstract speculation is closed to him. If he happens to want to make his contemporaries conscious of the moods stated above, his art should be called existential rather than existentialist. While most philosophers are, by nature, gifted writers, one might say that, properly speaking, there is no existentialist art.

2. EXISTENTIAL MOODS IN MODERN ART

Precisely for this reason, because existentialist philosophers make it their task to elucidate these moods through which—so they claim—our authentic situation in the Here and Now is revealed to us, they might perhaps help us to interpret the loud and inarticulate message of post-war art. It might be relevant at this point to recall what philosophies of existence have in common and, so far as possible, what particular feature in each of them might throw light on some aspect of modern art.

As we know, all of them start with the concrete situation of the self, as a center of reference, in the Here and Now. The personal or historical aspects of that situation are part of a human condition directly experienced through the moods stated above, which they try to elucidate. The feeling of absurdity is born out of the sense of absolute contingency (my being born here rather than there); the feeling of anguish is variously given as the sense of liberty facing that situation, or as the sense of a non-being which is part of the structure of liberty, or the background and the end of existence; the sense of guilt, whether interpreted as a consequence of the situation of the self as a center of reference, or as the sense of its finitude as it faces infinity, is connected with existence itself, rather than with some incidental psychic development. These themes are generally considered as belonging to religion rather than philosophy because, until recently, religion alone was expected to tell man something about the meaning of his concrete existence.

Some degree of discipline had to be acquired by the philosopher of existence before he could bring his consciousness to reflect on immediate subjective experiences. To the spirit of geometry which Descartes wants to bring to philosophy, Pascal opposes the intuitive spirit which consists in grasping a situation at once in its completeness. Modern existentialism generally resorts to intuition, or to Husserl's "phenomenological reduction," which consists in forgetting about the ultimate reality of things and concentrating on the structures of consciousness. These disciplines involve belief in a sort of immediate consciousness, which is not the subconscious but is implicit in the awareness of the object, and can be reflected upon, even though this process is most contrary to the natural trend of the human mind.

Furthermore, the philosophy of existence generally appears as a reaction against the prevalence of any sort of depersonalized philosophy or discipline. Thus, instead of starting, on the plane of contemplation, with the clear idea of Mind as thinking substance, Pascal starts with the direct apprehension of the Ego's concrete situation between two infinites of greatness and of smallness. On the plane of becoming, instead of starting like Hegel with the notion of the world as Idea, made up of Being and Non-Being, and realizing itself through history and through man, Kierkegaard shows man becoming himself face-to-face with God, whom he must answer every instant with "Yes" or "No." In our century, instead of starting with the notion of a creative evolution ending, on the plane of action, with *homo faber* conquering necessity by turning the objects of this world into a complex of tools, the existentialist starts with the situation of the individual self as a center of reference in this task of organization.

Furthermore, whether existentialism moves on the plane of contemplation, becoming, or action, or on all of these planes as the structure of human existence appears more complex, we can distinguish in all existentialist philosophics three fundamental levels, corresponding with the relations of the self to its object, to itself and other selves as subjects, and to some Absolute Subject. In Pascal, these three levels are the orders of bodies, mind, and Charity. In Kierkegaard, they are the aesthetic, the ethical, and the religious in its scandalous irrationality. It may help to throw light on some aspects of modern art to note that irony is like a stage between the aesthetic and the ethical insofar as it means rejection of the aesthetic, while humor is a stage between the ethical and the religious insofar as it constitutes the rejection of the conventional ethical. The strange humor of the dadaists and of Klee, among others, might be interpreted as a rejection of accepted ethical values.

The possibility of a contamination among the three planes, particularly the possibility of an objectification of the self, is a recurring theme in all forms of existentialism. This is most obvious in Buber's *I-It* and *I-Thou* planes, or in Marcel's *Having* as opposed to *Being*.

Also relevant is Jasper's insistence on those limiting, or extreme, situations which permit us to realize ourselves in failure as we pass from the plane of orientation to the plane of *Existenz* and from the plane of *Existenz* to the apprehension of its mysterious background of Transcendence. This notion of the revealing power of extreme situations, made only too familiar by the history of our times, was exploited in existentialist plays and fiction before it found its way into modern art, but the suggestion of agonizing situations has been so common in the painting of the last few decades that the popularity of this theme does not need being stressed here. The lingering dignity of the human figure, which the artist insists upon, even in his visions of suffering and decay may be explained in terms of the same philosophy.[2] We may stretch its meaning in sculpture and painting to find in it a feeling corresponding to Marcel's basic notion of "incarnation"; for in the suffering which they convey, we are reminded indeed of the fact that man does not simply *have* a body but *is* that body.

The mood which some other works reveal is more akin to Berdyaev's apocalyptic vision of an objectified world moving toward its end. Thus, not only representations of decaying flesh and of animal corpses stiffened by agony, but all sculptures laboriously contrived with clinkers, iron junk, and all the dead residues of a technological civilization seem to convey the same message. Berdyaev's prophetic announcement of the kingdom of the Spirit remains absent, however, from the field of art.

Heidegger's concept of authentic existence as being-for-death is strikingly illustrated by what may be called the apocalyptic aspect of modern art; but his notion of *Geworfenheit,* the feeling of having been thrown into the world without reason, the *ek-static* character of an existence which realizes itself by projecting itself in time and space, his picture of man as a "being of the horizon," all seem to me to have stronger affinities with the paintings of the surrealists, his contemporaries of the Thirties.

The works of Jean-Paul Sartre, being closer to the spirit of our post-war era and somewhat more analytical than those of his predecessors, might be of greater help in formulating the existential meaning of today's art. Sartre's main contribution to the philosophy of existence is, as we know, his conception of consciousness as perpetual negation, in fact as an absolute non-being which can only subsist as qualified negation of identity with its object. Thus, I am conscious of the picture in front of me insofar as I am conscious of not being the picture. Consciousness is always a mere presence to that which it is not. The object is really outside, for although it is only a series of appearances to me, that series can never be exhausted, which is probably what the cubists once tried to express; but my consciousness is lack of being and as such it is outside of the flux of causality, therefore free. It is up to me to select the picture as the object of my perception or to ignore it altogether. While my consciousness is turned toward the picture, it not only negates being the picture, but throws into a sort of non-being, as background, everything that is not the picture. The background has that sort of evanescent quality with which portrait painters used to surround their figures.

The picture, however, is more than an ordinary object: in itself it is nothing but canvas and pigment—this is probably the way a curious animal would look at it—but as the expression of another free consciousness, it has meaning and stands for a particular vision of the world which is proposed to me and which I am free to accept or to reject. Art then is more than mere expression, it is also a form of collaboration suggested by a free consciousness to another free consciousness. It is up to me to make the picture live on a symbolic plane which will be further defined later or to reject it as a plain object without meaning and therefore without value.

As proposing to me a particular vision of the world, the work of art does not essentially differ from the written work. In fact, the vision of the world suggested by Sartre's writings has much in common with that suggested by post-war art. Outside of man's freedom, the whole Sartrean universe is just there, totally contingent, unjustified, and therefore absurd, persisting in being, for no reason. Realization of its brute existence is experienced in nausea. While Sartre refers to brute existence as being-in-itself, we cannot fail to recognize in it a sort of dormant becoming, the objectified world of Berdyaev, the morass from which consciousness is trying to disentangle itself. Its entanglement is the very anti-value of consciousness, and this nauseating anti-value is precisely what modern art so felicitously manages to convey. The pure contingency of the body, deprived of the saving grace of its transcendence in the free act, is perfectly expressed through the artist's stress upon appropriate sections: massive trunks, bloated stomachs, withered limbs.

In Sartre's philosophy, realization of what causes nausea: the element of pure contingence in existence, is also its cancellation through the negative power of consciousness. Similarly, it has been advanced that the whole movement of modern art since World War II was a sort of catharsis:

> "These paintings," says Leon Golub of his own work, "attempt to reinstate a contemporary catharsis, that measure of man

which is related to an existential knowledge of the human condition. . . ." [3]

For the modern artist as for Sartre, there seems to be an obligation to assume the situation such as it is, before the situation can be transcended, surpassed, cancelled. What is the present situation to the sensitive consciousness of the artist? To quote Golub again: "Man is seen as having undergone a holocaust or facing annihilation or mutation." [4]

This is the situation; but, according to Sartre, a situation is to be realized in the light of a new situation to be created according to an ideal value. This ideal value, the grounding of being in consciousness, is not really accessible, except on the symbolic plane of art.

3. EXISTENTIAL SYMBOLISM IN MODERN ART: VALUES AND ANTI-VALUES

Outside the world of art, the things of this world appear as tools to be used for a purpose. But apart from their possible value as tools, they also appear with a symbolic meaning, as revealing certain ways of being; the qualities of things are particularly significant, and just as consciousness can single out an object from its background, it can single out qualities as possessing certain intrinsic ways of being. Textures, colors, fragrances have, according to Sartre, certain symbolic meanings which are the same for everybody. We are familiar with the meaning attached by Sartre to the rock as manifesting the permanency of being, to light as manifesting the transparency of consciousness, to water as manifesting the fluidity of time, freedom and change, to the viscous as manifesting that fluidity being absorbed by incipient thickness and opacity, a meaning which we implicitly recognize in its universality when we say that we are "swamped" with details. Colors also have meanings that we take for granted when we say that we are blue, or that somebody else is yellow, that we see red or that our prospects are black. What we do not clearly realize is that while these qualities have the same meaning for everybody, they may be anti-values to some and values to others or, if one prefers, that to some they represent ways of being to be avoided and to others ways of being to be sought or complacently accepted even though they go against a certain recognized set of human values.

What is true of life is also true of art. The use of clinkers in statuary, of sand, paper, and thread in painting, is therefore meaningful and legitimate from the viewpoint of existential symbolism. We should, however, be careful not to conclude that these textures represent values to the artist. They may symbolize a situation to be recognized as anti-value and rejected. The same is true of color and form. Art does not necessarily imply the formulation of new values; it may just as well constitute the formulation of anti-values.

Indeed, if we accept this existentialist notion of individual values attached to universal meanings inseparable from the qualities of things, we must consider art, not as the creation of values, but as a certain dimension of consciousness. I may be a representational painter of the traditional type, in search of a subject. Passing by a well-built house on perfectly landscaped grounds, I will think that I would love to live there, but I will look for my subject somewhere else, perhaps in some dismal, forsaken slum, after the taste of the ash-can school. Before the well-built house, I had felt that some other consciousness had been at work before me, the consciousness of the architect, and that there was nothing left for me to do; but this greenish sky above these crumbling brick walls is something no one has seen before, at least the way I see it. I can appropriate its desolate harmony and make it live in the minds of others, provided they are willing to follow me in this attempt. But today's art is way past the achievements of the ash-can school of painters still eager to offer some lingering touch of grace or beauty in desolate surroundings, to find values among anti-values. Modern art, since World War I, had certainly discovered a number of aesthetic values: the delicate vibration of colored greys in Klee, Picasso's challenging use of equally luminous colors partitioned with black, Braque's success in animating dull colors through contrast of warm and cold flat tones, clearly are aesthetic values tending toward harmony through resolution of an opposition; but since World War II, there has been an accelerated trend toward anti-values in art. This trend is apparent from the choice of subjects.

Regression toward animal forms or toward the childlike or the tribal, disintegration through the acceleration of unguided technology, and the apocalyptic vision have been the dominant themes. It would be futile to deny that the atmosphere of the cold war and the mood of preparation for atomic warfare have something to do with this. The artists themselves recognize the fact.[5] More sensitive than the rest of us, they seem to feel the need of making us conscious of some growing opacity of human conscious yielding to various forms of self-alienation. To that extent, their fight is that of the existentialists: a fight to oblige modern man to open his eyes and face the reality of his condition, as revealed by the present historical situation, so that he may act accordingly. If, as Sartre claims, each consciousness is an absolute; if therefore the basic relation between one consciousness and another is conflict and not "togetherness," some clear recognition of the fact might lead at least to some sense of reciprocity and team spirit; if undirected technology can lead only to total destruction, perhaps its dangers may profitably be suggested through the symbolism of art; if nature and creative evolution by themselves lead nowhere, at least the dangers of a possible regression toward a dormant sort of animal life should be concretely conveyed.

4. THE AESTHETIC, THE ARTISTIC, AND THE RELIGIOUS

The existentialist theologian Tillich, in his introduction to *New Images of Man,* states that what the artist seeks in "children's art, latrine art and what Dubuffet calls 'brute art,' is primarily the presence of 'a totemic image.' " We may, if we like, see in "brute art" the passage from the ethical to the religious plane of consciousness, the aesthetic plane being left far behind. Dubuffet himself, the chief exponent of the form of art in question, seems to confirm this view in the following remarks:

> *The slightest intervention of esthetics obstructs for me the efficiency of functioning* and spoils the sauce. That is why I try to reject from my works all that could have the smell of esthetics . . . *I have liked to carry the human image into a plane of seriousness where the futile embellishments of esthetics have no longer any place, onto a plane of high ceremony, of solemn office of celebration,* by helping myself with what Joseph Conrad calls: "a mixture of familiarity and terror," out of which the devotion is made which many religious minds offer to their gods and which does not, at times, exclude the use of swear words directed at them.[6]

Dubuffet admits that the terms "ugly" or "beautiful" are meaningless to him; If art, as I suggested above, is really the communication of a certain dimension of consciousness, there is no reason why art could not be anti-aesthetic. There is no reason either why art should not place itself at the service of a religious feeling and make it its duty to wage the fight of the religious against the aesthetic. André Malraux pointed out that if the sculptors of archaic Romanesque art did not convey the beauty of Greek human figures, it was not so much because the artist could not have done so but because to do so would have seemed a sin to him. The divorce of art from aesthetics is natural in an age which seeks new religious values.

We might perhaps wonder whether the "seriousness" of this quest is compatible with a form of humor that tries to detect the grotesque character of the human figure through the vision of a childlike mind. First of all, we should make a distinction between the "childish" and the "childlike." The "childlike," as opposed to the "childish," implies that very dimension of consciousness by which I tried to define the plane of art. What has become conscious in this form of art is a vision of man as a mechanical puppet, the depersonalized, interchangeable human being whom Heidegger calls *das man*. After the First World War, the German painter Grosz used the same technique to represent characters moved by elemental animal instincts and regressing into animal forms. No doubt the child, in a dim sort of way, sees grown-ups in this fashion: he would like to be able to look up to the grown-up as to a semi-divine consciousness in which he might find his justification, but as in Andersen's tale, no convention can make his pitiless eye see the emperor otherwise than naked.

The use of what Tillich calls latrine art, i.e., *graffiti* or wall scratches, follows somewhat the same pattern, but the wall scratch also symbolizes a sort of self-affirmation through negative behavior, an incipient rebellion against social conventions and order. Conscious use of the scratch technique—and of the unconventional representations it is generally used for—raises to the level of art what was merely a hopeless form of negative behavior.

Translated into post-existentialist terms, action painting itself is like the silent protest of the child, vigorously affirming the free negating function of consciousness by scratching a wall. The protest is there recorded in all its dynamism; the protest of action painting was already implicit in the expressive violence of abstractionism. In abstract impressionism, for instance, the illusion was conveyed at first sight that one was facing a representation so that the second look might, by surprise, plunge the beholder into the night of his own non-being, or into pure contingency, at his choice; but in action painting the protest against aesthetics is registered in its nakedness. Critics may try to see in such paintings the affirmation of a "new" form of aesthetics; their efforts go against the testimony of the artists themselves in most cases and against our own candid impressions in all others.

It would seem that after suggesting in all possible ways the possible disintegration of the world and of man, modern art was turning finally to the disintegration of art itself.

Existentialism may help us to understand our post-existentialist age, but it should be understood that a movement starting in the thirties should have run its normal course and that the following age, our own, should normally constitute a reaction against at least one aspect of existentialism. Let us place action painting in its cultural context. To the prevalence of the anti-novel (commonly understood as having nothing to say and saying it as boringly as possible), of the anti-theater (known in this country as the Theater of the Absurd, rich in social protest but at the expense of dramatic interest), of anti-poetry and, to some extent, of anti-architecture, corresponds the prevalence of what seems to be the challenge to art and the triumph of contingence rather than the unifying vision of the artist transcending his historical situation. But, if we admit that art is a dimension of consciousness independent of aesthetics, we can perfectly well understand the possibility of an art surrendering the aesthetic plane to make itself available for new ethical and religious values. Many thinkers have pointed out the resemblance between the apocalyptic vision in modern art and in similarly anguished periods of the past.

Since the past, however, does not repeat itself exactly, we have to place the latest manifestations of modern art in the context of the total contemporary situation in order to understand them.

First of all, it would serve no purpose at all to explain them merely through the urge of the individual artist; there have always been latrine art, childish art, and totem art. What is really meaningful is that these forms of "brute art" should be accepted as the representative art of our times. If we accept the existentialist concept of art as collaboration, on the plane of symbolism, between the artist and his contemporaries, we must admit that in the drama of modern art the decisive part was played by the juries who proposed it to the public and by the public itself, who accepted it as representative, despite some mild protest. But this picture will still be incomplete if we do not make the effort to place art in the context of the total historical situation.

There was great rejoicing among painters—and not merely among the "Fauves"—when the Mona Lisa was stolen from the Louvre early in this century. To the contemporaries of the Dadaïsts, after World War I, the Mona Lisa was only bearable with the addition of a pair of moustaches. In those days, museums were commonly referred to as the cemeteries of art, and the Italian Futurists advocated their total destruction. The spirit of cubism invaded fashions and mannerisms to a tyrannical degree. In our age, contemporary art is considered compatible with museum culture and with the revival of Gilbert and Sullivan musical comedies. The new image of man, and even more so of woman, from Tokyo to Los Angeles, is basically borrowed from Hollywood and not from modern art. Values are sought not only in the great arts of the past, more widely appreciated than ever before through circulating exhibits and colored reproductions, but also in such mass media as popular magazines and the cinema. It is from such mass media that our age derives its only aesthetic values, while modern art has assumed the responsibility of unveiling the dreadful and anguishing anti-values which constitute the other and equally real side of our situation.

The great misunderstanding about contemporary art stems from the fact that the public still insists in seeking new aesthetic values whereas the artist means to present what to him constitute the anti-values of our age. Perhaps when his somber message is better understood, a synthesis may come out of this opposition; but between now and then it would seem that the lingering influence of existentialism and the triumph of modern art may have led to a change in the religious sensibility of the people. Everything about modern art since World War II: its apocalyptic vision, its prophesies of human disintegration through unguided technology and regression into animal form, its grotesqueness, its somber irony and humor—qualities which, according to Kierkegaard always mark the passage from the aesthetic to the ethical and from the ethical to the religious—its very challenge of aesthetics would seem to correspond to an anguished quest for religious values grounded in full recognition of our historical situation.

If Tillich is right, the tribal doodling of the contemporary artist is the frenzied search of the totemic image, the unescapable idol which must serve as a new center of integration in the radiant City of the future; and this new idol, as Dubuffet asserts, is clearly the "human image" raised, as it is, grotesque, common, or pathetic, to the "high plane of seriousness where the futile embellishments of aesthetics have no longer any place, onto the plane of high ceremony, of solemn office of celebration."

Yet, one may wonder what this humanistic cult means.

Is it a distorted form of Christian *Agape,* akin to the Sartrean conception of man sacrificing himself to realize the ideal value of God, in himself and for himself, but unlike the Sartrean conception in championing anonymous man in his degradation and suffering, rather than the existentialist hero? Or is it a plain self-deification and anthropomorphic cult, rather than the critical presentation of man's situation which we have been trying to detect in the consciously "brute art" of to-day? It would seem to be both, since it is compounded of "the devotion . . . which many religious minds offer to their gods" and of "the use of swear words directed at them."

We have to accept today's art in its ambiguity, as a critical presentation of man with religious overtones, or as a religious quest with critical elements. Perhaps, at this point, the Bergsonian distinction between religion and mysticism as opposed to each other, yet constituting the two poles of a dialectical process, might help to clear matters. First and foremost an illustration of the humanistic phase of our post-existentialist era, today's art is more related to the quest of new religious values than to the mystical background which can be detected in existentialist philosophies.

NOTES

2 EXISTENTIALISM AND VITALISM

[1] A revised version of an article which appeared in French as "Des conceptions bergsonienne et sartrienne de la liberté," *French Review*, XXII, 2, Dec. 1948.

[2] *The Spirit of Modern Philosophy*, New York, Houghton, Mifflin & Co., 1896, p. 206.

[3] "The explanation of the world through becoming, conceived as a synthesis of being and non-being, is soon given, but has one reflected that the being in becoming could only be that synthesis if he were it [that synthesis] to himself in an act which would ground his own nothingness?" *L'Etre et le Néant* (cited hereafter as *EN*), Paris, Gallimard, 1943, p. 161. Unless specified otherwise, the translation is mine.

[4] *La Pensée et le mouvant*. Paris, Alcan, 1934, p. 123.

[5] *EN*, p. 47.

[6] *Ibid.*, p. 64.

[7] *Ibid.*, p. 64.

[8] *Ibid.*, p. 65.

[9] *Creative Evolution*, New York, Holt, 1924, p. 274.

[10] *Ibid.*, p. 296.

[11] *Ibid.*

[12] *EN*, p. 54.

[13] *Ibid.*, p. 66.

[14] *La Pensée et le mouvant*, p. 123.

[15] *EN*, p. 81.

[16] *Ibid.*, p. 156.

[17] *Ibid.*, p. 150.

[18] *Ibid.*, p. 154.

[19] *Ibid.*, p. 162.

[20] *Ibid.*, p. 167.

[21] *Ibid.*, p. 179.

[22] *La Pensée et le mouvant*, p. 191.

[23] *Ibid.*, p. 192.

[24] *Ibid.*, p. 207.

[25] *Ibid.*, p. 208.

[26] *EN*, p. 360.

[27] *Ibid., loc. cit.*

[28] *Ibid.*, p. 278.

[29] *Ibid.*, p. 709.

[30] Bergson, *Les deux sources de la morale et de la religion.* Paris, Alcan, 1932, p. 343.

[31] *The Creative Mind*, New York, Philosophical Library, 1946, p. 92.

[32] *Creative Evolution*, p. 247.

[33] *Ibid.*, pp. 270–271.

[34] *La Nausée*, Paris, Gallimard, 1938, p. 23 (Cited hereafter as *LN*). Unless specified otherwise, the translation is mine.

[35] *Ibid.*, p. 24.

[36] *Ibid.*, p. 168.

[37] *Ibid.*, p. 29.

3 EXISTENTIALISM AND HUMANISM

[1] *Soliloquies*, II, i. I.

[2] Etienne Gilson, "The Future of Augustinian Metaphysics," in M. C. D'Arcy (ed.), *St. Augustine*, Meridian Books, World Publishing Co., Cleveland, 1961, p. 295.

[3] "Tanta est tamen cogitationis vis, ut nec ipsa mens quodammodo se in conspectu suo ponat, nisi se cogitat": *De Trinitate*, XIV, 6, 8, t. 42, c. 1041, 1092, quoted by Gilson, *Introduction à l'Etude de Saint Augustin*, Paris, Vrin, 1949, p. 293.

[4] *Pensées*, Everyman's Library, London, 1931. 77, p. 23.

[5] *De Genisi ad litteram*, XII, xvii, 33, quoted by D'Arcy, "The Philosophy of St. Augustine," *op. cit.*, p. 176.

[6] D'Arcy, *op. cit.*, p. 182.

[7] *Anim.*, X, xiii, quoted by D'Arcy, *op. cit.*, p. 191.

[8] D'Arcy, *op. cit.*, p. 191.

[9] *The Essayes of Montaigne*, Florio's translation, Modern Library, New York, 1933, Third Book, XIII, p. 1013 (italics mine).

[10] *Loc. cit.*, p. 1007.

[11] *Pensées*, 72, p. 17.

[12] *Ibid.*, 72, p. 19.

[13] *Ibid.*

[14] *Ibid.*, 205, p. 61.

[15] *Ibid.*, 206, p. 61.

[16] *Ibid.*, 72, p. 21.

[17] *Ibid.*, 82, p. 25.

[18] *Ibid.*, 82, p. 26.
[19] *Ibid.*, 82, p. 25.
[20] *Op. cit.*, 2d Book, XII, p. 538 (italics mine).
[21] *Pensées*, 88, p. 28.
[22] *Ibid.*, 92, p. 19.
[23] *Ibid.*, 93, p. 29.
[24] *Ibid.*, 99, p. 36.
[25] *Ibid.*, 455, p. 127 (italics mine).
[26] *Ibid.*, 147, p. 45.
[27] *The Maxims*, translated by FitzGibbon, Allan Wingate, London, 1957. 564, p. 144.
[28] *Ibid.*, 564, pp. 145–146.
[29] *Ibid.*, 564, p. 145.
[30] *Ibid.*, 564, p. 146.
[31] *Ibid.*, pp. 147–148 (italics mine).
[32] *Ibid.*, 608, p. 159.
[33] *Treatise on Passions*, 3d Part, Art. 102–109.
[34] *LN*, p. 174.
[35] *Op. cit.*, 194, p. 55.
[36] *Ibid.*, 199, p. 60.
[37] *Ibid.*, 139, p. 39.
[38] *Ibid.*, 139, p. 40.
[39] *Ibid.*, 139, p. 41.
[40] *Ibid.*, 139, p. 42.
[41] *Ibid.*
[42] *Ibid.*, 139, p. 41.
[43] *Ibid.*, 172, p. 50.
[44] *Ibid.*, 171, p. 49.
[45] *Ibid.*, 347, p. 97.
[46] *Ibid.*, 344, p. 96.
[47] *Ibid.*, 347, p. 97.
[48] *Ibid.*, 397, p. 107.
[49] *Ibid.*, 400, p. 197.
[50] *Ibid.*, 404, p. 108.
[51] *Ibid.*, 409, 109.
[52] *Ibid.*, 358, p. 99.
[53] *Ibid.*, 70, p. 16.
[54] *Ibid.*, 413, p. 109.
[55] *Ibid.*, 430, pp. 115–116.

4 THE SCANDAL OF MULTIPLICITY OF CONSCIOUSNESSES

[1] A. de Waelhens, *La philosophie de Martin Heidegger*, Louvain, Editions de l'Institut supérieur de philosophie, 1942, p. 163. (The translation is mine.)
[2] *EN*, p. 238.
[3] The idea of scandal, as an existential datum, has received various explanations: In Kierkegaard, the scandal is the religious element which transcends reason and must be placed above reason. The example given is that of Abraham

ready to sacrifice his son on God's order; scandal is also found in the notion of God made man and killed by man. Le Senne defines scandal as a provoking determination the intentional meaning of which is an attack, previously instigated between a value and a self. (Le Senne, "Le Scandale," in *L'Existence*, Paris, Gallimard, 1945, p. 141.) Gilson, like Sartre, establishes a direct connection between scandal and the existence of the other, but purely on the intellectual plane: "What remains scandalous for analytic thought, in efficient causality is . . . the apparition of another existent starting from a certain existent. . . ." (Gilson, "Limites de la philosophie," *ibid.*, p. 75.) Finality surging from causality through the other's existence does not, however, imply the constitution of a totalitarian world with the other as a center of reference. In all cases, scandal is an attack against a fundamental value.

[4] *EN*, p. 356.

[5] J-P. Sartre, *Théâtre*, Paris, Gallimard, 1947, p. 17.

[6] *Ibid.*, p. 136.

[7] *Ibid.*, p. 137.

[8] *Ibid.*, p. 138.

[9] *Ibid.*, p. 139.

[10] *Ibid.*, p. 140.

[11] *Ibid.*, p. 158.

[12] *Ibid.*, p. 164.

[13] *Le Sursis*, Gallimard, 1945, p. 160.

[14] *Ibid.*, p. 158.

[15] Simone de Beauvoir, *Le Sang des autres*, Paris, Gallimard, 1947, p. 115.

[16] Simone de Beauvoir, *L'Invitée*, Paris, Gallimard, 1943, p. 301.

[17] *Ibid.*, p. 311.

[18] *Ibid.*, p. 303.

[19] *Ibid.*, p. 312.

[20] J-P. Sartre, *Théâtre*, p. 108.

[21] *Le Sang des autres*, p. 224.

[22] Simone de Beauvoir, *Pour une morale de l'ambiguité*, Paris, Gallimard, 1947, p. 99.

[23] *Ibid.*, p. 101.

[24] *Ibid.*, p. 222.

[25] *Ibid.*, p. 183.

[26] *Ibid.*, p. 183.

[27] *EN*, pp. 497–498.

[28] This essay, published in French as *Le Scandale de la Multiplicité des consciences chez Huxley, Sartre et Simone de Beauvoir*, in *Symposium*, V, 2, Nov., 1951, included a section bearing on the mystical implications of the subject; these are treated in my essay *"That Art Thou Not": Existentialism and Mysticism*.

5 EXISTENTIAL SYMBOLISM

[1] ". . . human reality, long before it can operate as *libido* or will-to-power, is choice of being, either directly or through appropriation of the world." *EN*, p. 693.

[2] "While the desire to be bears directly on the for-itself and projects to confer on it without intermediary the dignity of being in-itself-for-itself, the desire to have aims at the for-itself on, in, and through the world." *Ibid.*, p. 689.

[3] "One sees that appropriation is nothing else than the *symbol* of the ideal of the for-itself, or value. The couple for-itself possessing and in-itself possessed has value only for the being who is merely so that he may possess himself, and whose possession is its own creation, i.e. God. . . ." *Ibid.*, p. 687.

[4] *Ibid.*, p. 687.

[5] *Ibid.*, p. 686.

[6] *Ibid.*, p. 690.

[7] *Ibid.*, p. 696.

[8] *Ibid.*, p. 704.

[9] The *Lusher Test*, Test-Verlag, Basel, 1949, based on the theory developed by Dr. Max Lusher's *Psychologie des Farben*, claims to determine the reaction pattern of an individual in a given life situation according to his reactions before various colors, or shades of the same colors. It is interesting to note that the meanings attached to colors in this test are very nearly the same as in Sartre, and that the same stress is laid on the voluntaristic aspect of the patterns of behavior revealed by the test.

[10] *EN*, p. 671.

[11] *Ibid.*, p. 668.

[12] *Ibid.*, p. 702.

[13] *Ibid.*, p. 699.

[14] *Ibid.*, *loc. cit.*

[15] *Ibid.*, p. 701.

[16] *EN*, p. 702.

[17] *Ibid.*, p. 701. Cf., on the biological plane, images used by Bergson to describe the way in which creative evolution becomes imprisoned by its very realizations: with him, however, "solidification" or "ossification," not "viscosity," symbolizes this process. In both cases, however, we are dealing with a progressive loss of liberty.

[18] J-P. Sartre, *L'Age de Raison*, Paris, Gallimard, 1945, p. 268. (Cited hereafter as *LADR*.)

[19] *LS*, p. 286.

[20] *LADR*, p. 275.

[21] *LS*, p. 226.

[22] J-P. Sartre, *Le Mur*, Paris, Gallimard, 1947, p. 203. (Cited hereafter as *LM*.)

[23] *LS*, p. 285.

[24] *Ibid.*, p. 285.

[25] J-P. Sartre, *La Mort dans l'âme*, Paris, Gallimard, 1949, p. 42. (Cited hereafter as *LMDLA*.)

[26] *Ibid.*, p. 177.

[27] *Ibid.*, p. 129.

[28] *Ibid.*, p. 177.

[29] *LMDLA*, p. 9.

[30] *Ibid.*, p. 79.

[31] *LS*, p. 196.

[32] *Intimité, LM*, p. 105.

[33] *LADR*, p. 53.

[34] *Ibid.*

[35] *Ibid.*, p. 96.

[36] *LN*, p. 23.

[37] *LADR*, p. 275.

[38] *LS*, pp. 107–109.

[39] *Intimité, LM*, p. 122.

[40] *Ibid.*, p. 131.

[41] *LADR*, p. 168.

[42] *LMDLA*, p. 116.

[43] *LS*, p. 288.

[44] *Ibid.*, p. 72.

[45] *LADR*, p. 190.

[46] *LN*, p. 31.

[47] *Ibid.*, p. 207.

[48] *Ibid.*, p. 208.

[49] *LADR*, p. 144.

[50] *LADR*, p. 132. Cf. on the symbolic meaning of colors, the curious chapter on Antonin Artaud's theory, in J-L. Barrault's *Reflexions sur le Théâtre*, Paris, Vautrain, 1949, p. 66. Correspondences between colors and behavior are given as follows: blue: to give; purple: to exchange; red: to receive; orange: to keep; yellow: to maintain; green: to reject.

[51] *Ibid.*, p. 129. I follow Stuart Gilbert's translation fairly closely here.

[52] *LMDLA*, p. 26.

[53] *LS*, p. 72.

[54] *LADR*, p. 11.

[55] Cf. above, note 23.

[56] Sartre, *Théâtre*, p. 18.

[57] Cf. above, note 38.

[58] *EN*, p. 691.

[59] *LMDLA*, p. 116.

[60] *LADR*, p. 55.

[61] *LS*, p. 210.

[62] *LMDLA*, p. 45.

[63] *Ibid.*, p. 168.

[64] *Ibid.*, p. 174.

[65] *L'Enfance d'un chef, LM*, p. 170.

[66] *LN*, p. 225.

[67] *Ibid.*, p. 37.

[68] *Ibid., loc. cit.*

[69] *LADR*, pp. 191–192.

[70] *LN*, p. 131.

[71] *LADR*, p. 53.

[72] J-P. Sartre, *The Psychology of Imagination*, New York, Philosophical Society, 1948, p. 160.

[73] *LADR*, p. 93.

[74] *Ibid.*, p. 268.

[75] *L'Enfance d'un chef, LM,* p. 192.
[76] *LADR,* p. 198.
[77] *Ibid.,* p. 18.
[78] *Ibid.,* p. 168.
[79] *LMDLA,* p. 116.

6 "THAT ART THOU NOT": EXISTENTIALISM AND MYSTICISM

[1] William James, *The Varieties of Religious Experience,* London, New York, Longmans, Green & Co., 1913, p. 499.
[2] *Ibid., loc. cit.*
[3] *Ibid.,* p. 489.
[4] *Ibid.,* p. 499.
[5] *Ibid.,* p. 500.
[6] R. Otto, *Mystique d'Orient et Mystique d'Occident,* Paris, Payot, 1951, p. 261. (The translation from the French text, somewhat more precise than the English text, is mine.)
[7] *Op. cit.,* p. 513.
[8] *Ibid.,* p. 581.
[9] *Ibid.,* p. 419.
[10] Otto, *op. cit.,* p. 261.
[11] *Ibid.,* p. 63.
[12] Somerset Maugham, *The Razor's Edge,* Philadelphia, Blakiston Co., 1944, p. 218.
[13] *Ibid.,* p. 220.
[14] Otto, *op. cit.,* p. 257.
[15] E. Brehier, *Ennéades,* Paris, Les Belles Lettres, p. 115, quoted by Otto, *op. cit.,* p. 58.
[16] Aldous Huxley, *Eyeless in Gaza,* Chatto & Windus, London, 1950, p. 615 (italics mine).
[17] D. T. Suzuki, *Selected Writings,* ed. by William Barrett, New York, Doubleday, 1956, p. 191.
[18] James, *op. cit.,* p. 416.
[19] Quoted by James, *ibid.,* pp. 416–417.
[20] *Ibid.,* p. 437.
[21] *Ibid., loc cit.*
[22] Otto, *op. cit.,* p. 101.
[23] *Ibid.,* p. 104.
[24] Maugham, *op. cit.,* p. 215.
[25] Otto, *op. cit.,* p. 102.
[26] *Ibid.,* p. 101.
[27] Otto, *op. cit.,* p. 221.
[28] *Obermann,* Letter XXX, quoted by James, *op. cit.,* p. 477.
[29] Henri Niel, *De la Mediation dans la Philosophie de Hegel,* Paris, Aubier, 1945, p. 57. (Translations from that work are mine.)
[30] Quoted by Niel, *op. cit.,* p. 41.
[31] *Ibid.,* p. 79.
[32] *Ibid.,* p. 46.

[33] Niel, *op. cit.*, p. 47.

[34] "Existentialism," in the *History of Philosophical Systems*, ed. Vergilius Ferm, Ames, Iowa, Littlefield, Adams & Co., 1958, p. 406.

[35] James Collins, *The Existentialists, a Critical Study*, Chicago, Henry Regnery, 1932. See heading of his chapter on Sartre.

[36] Gabriel Marcel, *Etre et Avoir*, Paris, Aubier, 1935, p. 119.

[37] Nicolas Berdiaeff, *Dialectique existentielle du divin et de l'humain*, Paris, J. B. Janin, p. 14.

[38] *Ibid.*, p. 143.

[39] *The Beginning and the End*, New York, Harper, 1952, p. 137.

[40] *Etre et Avoir*, p. 119.

[41] *Dialectique existentielle du divin et de l'humain*, p. 26.

[42] *Ibid.*, *loc. cit.*

[43] S. de Beauvoir, *Les Mémoires d'une jeune fille rangée*, Paris, Gallimard, p. 340.

[44] *EN*, p. 361.

[45] *Ibid.*, p. 362.

[46] *Ibid.*, p 363.

[47] *Ibid.*, *loc. cit.*

[48] *Ibid.*, *loc. cit.*

[49] See note 27.

[50] In *Mysticism and the Modern Mind*, ed. A. P. Sternotte, New York, Liberal Press, p. 35.

[51] Quoted from the Lloyd Alexander translation, Norfolk, 1949, p. 180, in *Mysticism and the Modern Mind*, p. 35.

[52] *Ibid.*, p. 148.

[53] *Ibid.*, p. 92.

[54] Henry Babel, *La Pensée d'Albert Schweitzer*, Neuchatel, Messeiller, p. 208.

[55] *Ibid.*, p. 55.

[56] *Les Mots*, in *Les Temps modernes*, Oct., Nov., 1963.

[57] *Mysticism and the Modern Mind*, pp. 149–150.

7   EXISTENTIALISM AND MARXISM

[1] J-P. Sartre, *Critique de la raison dialectique* (précédé de *Question de méthode*) Tome I, Paris, Gallimard, 1960. "Matérialisme et Révolution" was first published by *Les Temps modernes*, Vol. I, Nos. 9 and 10, June–July 1946. It appears in translation as Chapter 13 of Sartre's *Literary and Philosophical Essays*, New York, Criterion Books, 1955.

[2] "The theory of knowledge . . . remains the weak point of Marxism." *Critique de la raison dialectique* (cited hereafter as *CRD*), p. 30, note 1. (Translations from this work are mine.)

[3] I quote freely from my own summary in *To Be and Not To Be: An Analysis of Jean-Paul Sartre's Ontology*, Detroit, Wayne State University Press, 1962, pp. 145–146.

[4] Walter Odajnyk, *Marxism and Existentialism*, New York, Doubleday, 1965, p. 21.

[5] *Ibid.*, p. 24.

[6] *Ibid.*, p. 27.

[7] *Ibid.*, p. 41

[8] *Marx & Engels*, in *Basic Writings of Politics & Philosophy*, ed. Lewis S. Feuer, Doubleday, 1959, pp. 47–50. (The term "qual" is not italicized in the text.)

[9] *Ibid.*, p. 75

[10] *Ibid.*, p. 81

[11] *Ibid.*, p. 82.

[12] *Ibid.*, p. 83.

[13] This matter is summed up as follows by a disciple of de Broglie:

"Einstein . . . was able to declare that electro-magnetic waves (light) propel themselves in a space completely empty. We know of liquid waves, air waves, etc., but we are dealing here with the waves of a 'non-being.' *The void does exist.*

"But this is not all. According to the wave mechanics of M. de Broglie, which proved correct beyond discussion, this void is not only the medium of electro-magnetic waves but also of electronic waves, i.e. the electron is the wave of something which is a non-being. Moreover, a pair of electrons, positive and negative, can create itself, or emerge, from this void, and immerse itself, and annihilate itself in this void. *Nothing nihilates.* If one carries this theory to its extreme logical consequence, one can show that each time there is an electric charge, the void around it *polarizes* itself, i.e., that a great number of pairs of positive and negative electrons emerge from the void and produce a definite charge opposed to the charge which has been brought there. *Non-being reacts.*

"Thus we must say that the void in modern physics is not a simple negation of all being. It is rather an immense reservoir of all being in a latent, dormant, entirely neutralized form. Without void, nothing can exist. The void is at the same time the negation of being and being itself." Michael Satosi Watanabe, "L'Etre et le Non-Etre en physique atomistique." *Thélème,* Wayne State University III, 1, April 1954. (My translation, italics mine.)

[14] *Marx & Engels, op. cit.,* p. 88.

[15] Odajnyk, *op. cit.,* p. 98.

[16] "Dühring's Revolution in Science," *Marx & Engels, op. cit.,* p. 279.

[17] *Ibid.,* p. 279.

[18] *Ibid.,* p. 411.

[19] *Ibid.,* p. 12.

[20] *CRD,* p. 23.

[21] *Ibid.,* p. 31.

[22] *EN,* p. 361.

[23] Desan, *op. cit.,* p. 140.

[24] *CRD,* p. 388.

[25] Desan, *op. cit.,* p. 187.

[26] Europa-Verlag AG., Wien, 1964; Fisher Bücherei, Frankfurt, Hamburg, 1966. "Die These, dass die Menschen ihre Geschichte auf Grund gegebener Bedingungen machen, führt *nicht* zur Negierung des historischen Determinismus,

sondern zur spezifischen Interpretation des Mechanismus, gemäss welchem dieser Determinismus arbeitet." p. 42. Schaff's conclusions will be found in Odajnyk, *op. cit.*, p. 141.

[27] Available as Political Letter, New Series, No. 7, *N&L*, 8751 Grand River, Detroit 4, Mich.

[28] Odajnyk, *op. cit.*, p. 170.

8 CONCLUSION: A FAREWELL

[1] Cf. Madeleine Chapsal, "To Show, To Demonstrate . . . ," *Yale French Studies*, Thirty, 1963, p. 36.

[2] Joseph H. McMahon, "A Reader's Hesitations," *Ibid.*, p. 106.

APPENDIX: EXISTENTIALISM AND POST-WAR ART, 1945–1960

[1] A paper read before the Society of Women Painters, Detroit, Michigan, in May, 1963.

[2] "In the painting of Buchenwald and Dachau I wanted to express the belief that the human image, even when disfigured by the executioner, is grand in meaning. No brutality will ever cancel that meaning. Painting may increase it by changing what is disfigured into what is transfigured. . . ." Rico Lebrun, quoted in Peter Selz, *New Images of Man*, New York, Doubleday, 1959, p. 99. Cited hereafter as *NIOM*.

[3] *NIOM*, p. 76.

[4] *Ibid.*

[5] "After all, there is an atom bomb, a world in turmoil. . . ." De Kooning, quoted in *NIOM*, p. 92.

"At first we cannot see beyond the path that leads downwards to 'dark and hateful things'—but no light or beauty will ever come from the man who cannot bear the sight." C. G. Jung, quoted in *NIOM*, p. 134.

[6] *NIOM*, p. 61 (italics mine).

INDEX

Index

Jacques L. Salvan, professor emeritus of French, Wayne State University, now devotes his time to traveling, writing and lecturing. He is the author of *Le Romantisme français l'Angleterre victorienne* (1949) and *To Be and Not to Be* (Wayne State University Press, 1962).

The manuscript was prepared for publication by Barbara Woodward. The book was designed by Richard Kinney. The type faces used are Linotype Granjon and Alternate Gothic.

The book is printed on Glatfelter's Old Forge and bound in Columbia Mills Bayside Vellum. Manufactured in the United States of America.